PRAISE FOR QUICKSILVER

Against the backdrop of the most significant global economic meltdown since the Great Depression, Dr. O'Brien presents a compelling argument for America's leaders to stop relying on their experience to solve problems and begin mastery of conscious leadership.

—EDWARD BURGHARD
Executive Director, Ohio Business Development Coalition
CEO, The Burghard Group LLC

Quicksilver presents an atypical roadmap for creating desirable change. It's called "consciousness." In an excellent, easy-to-read narrative, Dr. O'Brien teaches it in a way that helps leaders free themselves from inevitable unconscious illusions that trap us all.

—IDA CRITELLI SCHICK, Ph.D., M.S., FACHE
Professor and Chair, Dept. of Health Services Admin.
Xavier University

On your journey through this book, you will learn from real stories and come away with real wisdom.

—HY POMERANCE, Ph.D., Head of Talent Development
New York Life Insurance Company

Michael O'Brien offers not useful excuses, but insights and help in becoming more accountable and happier in personal and work life.

—SR. CAROL KEEHAN, DC, President and CEO
The Catholic Health Association

Quicksilver marries behavior theory with business practice in a unique and readable way featuring conscious creativity and personal responsibility. It couldn't be more timely and relevant.

—GEORGE MANNING, Professor
Dept. of Psychological Science, Northern Kentucky University

Michael has given those of us in the trenches of the efforts to improve healthcare the most valuable tool I've yet seen.

—RANDY RANDOLPH, M.D.
Chief Medical Officer, Catholic Healthcare Partners

Quicksilver is a must read for people who want to break out of the ordinary and become transformational leaders.

—KAREN PUCKETT
COO, CenturyLink

Dr. O'Brien has a knack for cutting through psychobabble to provide clear and concise examples of the emotional barriers that often cause leaders to miss important signals.

—MARVIN P. MITCHELL
Chair, Division of Media Support Services, Mayo Clinic

Two sentences make this book worth its price to me: 1) "So if you habitually declare breakdowns to be caused by others who aren't doing, according to your personal narrative, what they should do, then there is no question for your mind to answer, no problem for it to solve." And 2) "To declare that something should not be a certain way is life's ultimate whine." I am going to look for ways to include Quicksilver principles in my teaching.

—WILLIAM STIMSON, Ph.D.
Director, Journalism Program, Eastern Washington University

Larry Shook and I were crewchiefs in the same helicopter gunship platoon in Vietnam. His epilogue captures what that was like, and both of us experienced superb leadership in circumstances when our lives were at risk. When the book arrived I was mired in a personal crisis that had been brewing for years. There seemed to be no resolution. So I tried one of Michael O'Brien's exercises (Shoulds versus Coulds) and the situation changed immediately.

—FRANS VANDENBROEK, VP Regulatory Affairs
Applied Medical Resources, Rancho Santa Margarita, Calif.

Quicksilver is a perfect complement for the wide range of books "about" leadership. This book offers clear guidance for becoming a leader that can effectively and consistently execute the strategies other books theorize about.

—GORDON BARNHART
Center for Heroic Leadership

This book not only engages the imagination, it offers leadership tools that work. A must read for every leader!

—JON C. ABELES
Senior Vice President, Catholic Healthcare Partners

A no-nonsense, very readable guide to help executives and their boards of directors become honest with themselves and quickly get their management teams and institutions on the mend.

—MICHAEL FORDNEY, Director
BMO Capital Markets

The work of personal emotional surveillance laid out in this book isn't for the feint of heart. As leaders, we have a choice to make, to lead out of habit or to lead intentionally.

—TAMMIE MCMANN BRAILSFORD
COO, MemorialCare Health System

Having had the opportunity to read many leadership developement and executive coaching books and articles, I think this book is the best. The wisdom, insights and practical applications will be of great value to my clients, now more than ever. In addition, I am certain to apply this reading in both my work and personal life. Thank you for this contribution.

—JIM GAUSS,
CEO, Witt/Kieffer

Quicksilver is an owner's manual for the grey matter between your ears. Michael O'Brien and Larry Shook show how leaders who fail to reflect on their thinking during times of adversity are dangerous to themselves and their organizations.

—BILL PASMORE. Sr. VP
Organizational Practice Leader, Center for Creative Leadership

Habitual thinking creates blind spots and limits a leader's ability to solve today's complex problems. Quicksilver provides several practices that enable a leader to not only recognize those blind spots but also develop new habits, which lead to improved performance.

—ELAINE HOLLAND
Chief Talent Officer, Millward Brown

The economic debacle of the 21st century's first decade is an elegant lens in which to reflect on the nature of true leadership, and how our leaders let us down. Real leadership requires intellectual honesty and rigor, paying attention to the right things, connection to higher values, courage, and decisive action. All these themes of leadership and recent history are brilliantly explored in Quicksilver.

—NEIL STROUL, Ph.D., Founding Faculty Member
Georgetown University Leadership Coaching Program

Quicksilver is a fascinating exposé of why we behave the way we do and what we can do to adapt our behavior, our leadership, our approach to relationships.

—JANE CROWLEY, EVP, CAO
Catholic Healthcare Partners

Quicksilver is an inspiring read for both established and novice leaders. Dr. Michael O'Brien offers a critical and sound analysis of the all-too-human emotional and cognitive blind spots that impair the effectiveness of leaders.
—RICHARD G. AZIZKHAN, MD, PhD (Hon)
Surgeon-in-Chief, Cincinnati Children's Hospital Medical Center
Professor of Surgery and Pediatrics, University of Cincinnati College of Medicine

Loved the book. It resonated, and I like the writing style. I could hear Michael's and Mark's voices as I read through it.
—DEBBIE BLOOMFIELD
CFO, Mercy Health Partners, Southwest Ohio

The hours spent with Quicksilver will be richly rewarded in your work and personal life, especially if you implement the many wise practices the authors suggest. Both practical and passionate, O'Brien believes in the possibility of change and helps you believe it too.
—DORIS GOTTEMOELLER, RSM
SVP for Mission and Values Integration, Catholic Healthcare Partners

A very clear, concise guide to improving one's leadership skills. Theoretically grounded and yet powerful in its application. This is more than a book for business.
—MARK JAEGER
Engineering manager at one of the world's
largest consumer products companies

Relevant examples of how even the best and brightest become unconscious! Solid, practical advice of how to always stay relevant, conscious and effective.
—RICHARD PONTIN
Tangoe, Inc.

Quicksilver addresses what Martin Luther King referred to as "The fierce urgency of now." It is not simply about formal leadership; it is about being fully aware in an unprecedented time of change and opportunity.
—DENNIS TIRMAN
Tirman Consulting, LLC

I know from personal experience that Michael O'Brien's approach [to leadership coaching] creates real breakthroughs and results for individuals and teams unlike anything else I have ever seen.
—ANNA PHILLIPS
Senior Partner and Board Chair, Witt/Kieffer

QUICKSILVER

A Revolutionary Way
to Lead the Many
and the Few—
Beginning with YOU

_____

MICHAEL O'BRIEN, Ed.D.
and LARRY SHOOK

SOMBRERO PRESS
SPOKANE, WASHINGTON

sOMBRERo
P R E S S

an imprint of
THE PRINTED WORD INC.
Spokane, Washington

Library of Congress Cataloging-in-Publication Data

O'Brien, Michael J. (Michael James), 1953-
Quicksilver : a revolutionary way to lead the many and the few—beginning with you / by Michael O'Brien and Larry Shook.
  p. cm.
Includes bibliographical references.
ISBN 978-1-934738-21-4 (pbk. : alk. paper)
  1.   Leadership—Psychological aspects. 2.   Decision making—Psychological aspects. 3.   Problem solving. I. Shook, Larry. II. Title.
BF637.L4O27 2010
158—dc22

                    2009038650

ISBN-13: 978-1-934738-21-4
ISBN-10: 1-934738-21-2

First Printing January 2010
10 9 8 7 6 5 4 3 2

Printed in the United States of America

Book Design: Dotti Albertine

The corporate mission of The Printed Word Inc.: *inform, uplift & empower*

For my clients
who constantly inspire me
with the power and dedication
of their quicksilver work,
for my colleagues
who help them do it,
and for my wife and children.
—MICHAEL O'BRIEN

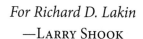

For Richard D. Lakin
—LARRY SHOOK

ACKNOWLEDGMENTS

I AM INDEBTED beyond the capability of repayment
to many people who have contributed to my personal
and professional development. In many ways, my life
is like a beautiful tapestry whose individual threads
wouldn't have foretold the current picture of my life.
But I would like to acknowledge in particular the
following organizations and individuals who were and
are instrumental in my development: Fr. Ray Holtz,
National Training Laboratories (NTL), Werner Erhard,
Dr. Howard Johnston, Jan Smith and the Center for
Authentic Leadership, and Beverly Outcalt O'Brien.
—MO'B

IN EVERY RESPECT I owe my life to three women: My
mother, Dorothy May Shook; my aunt Mary Cecile
Smith; my wife and editor, Judy Laddon, who "sees"
Quicksilver as Michael and I do. —LS

CONTENTS

FOREWORD *by Michael D. Connelly*   **xvii**

INTRODUCTION   **xxi**
Invitation to the Reinventors' Ball
The nuclear reactor at your desk

CHAPTER ONE   **1**
Wall Street's Monster
The wages of unconscious leadership

CHAPTER TWO   **31**
The Way We Are
The world changes the brain, then the brain returns
the favor and changes the world. Who's in charge?

Instruction Manual   **55**
The Angel in the Stone: A Quicksilver chisel set
for continuously discovering, and displaying,
your best self

CHAPTER THREE   **65**
Be Absolutely Accountable
The surprising source of true freedom

CHAPTER FOUR   81
Be (Really) Brave
The world's terrible lie about courage

CHAPTER FIVE   101
Be Authentic
The Cliff Notes on trustworthiness

CHAPTER SIX   121
Be Brilliantly Intentional
The beacon within can cut through any darkness.
Here's how to use it.

CHAPTER SEVEN   153
Create the Truth
The mind invents reality, and then says,
"I didn't do it."

CHAPTER EIGHT
The Discreet Charm of the Honest Mess
A lesson from baseball   175

CHAPTER NINE
2.7 Seconds
Bull-riding requires a fire in the belly.
So does Quicksilver leadership   195

EPILOGUE   **207**
Captain Ski
A personal memory of a great leader amidst great
confusion

Quicksilver Quickly   **217**
   Three Simple Steps
   Quicksilver Principles
   List of Practices

Authors' Bios   **221**

LIST OF PRACTICES

ACCOUNTABILITY   77
Change Shoulds to Coulds
Don't let the past determine your future

COURAGE
Breathe
Oxygen fuels your emotional intelligence   94

Tell Yourself a Story
Take charge of your mind's greatest power   96

AUTHENTICITY
Evaluate a Stuck Relationship   117
Navigate beyond your fear toward your principles

Be Complete with Incompletion   118
Live well, with some things unfinished

INTENTIONALITY
Discover Your Defensive Routines: 143
Fight & Flight
Learn to notice when you've been hijacked

Have a Breakthrough Conversation   146
See the other person's story

Scout for Organizational Defensive Routines   148
Discuss (gulp) the unmentionable

Move Beyond Bad Moods, Quickly   150
Notice and lay down your burdens

CREATE THE TRUTH
Keep a "Snake List"   167
Awareness and good technique stop your
problems from biting you

Be Interested vs. Interesting   168
Really, try it. You'll become interesting

Turn Complaints Into Requests   168
End a lot of suffering

Depose Ideology   169
Taking a stand is way more powerful

Explore the Heart of Conflict with   171
Constructive Dialogue
Develop a nimble mind that creates empathy

CAPITALIZE ON MESSES
Ask Yourself a "Paradoxical   187
Development Question"
Unleash the *über* problem-solver within

Ask Yourself What You Need   189
Illuminate your secret yearnings so you can get
them met

Ask for Forgiveness
Liberate yourself from past mistakes   191

Ask Yourself the Biggest Question of All
When you know the answer, you can truly lead   192

FOREWORD

IN MY EXPERIENCE an occupational hazard of leadership is that it tends to build up overconfidence in our own thought processes. Leaders often believe that they have gotten to where they are because they know how to analyze things better than others.

As this book shows, our country is replete with recognized leaders who have succumbed to this hazard and unintentionally led their own organizations into catastrophe. Better than any book I know, *Quicksilver* exposes the cause of this tendency, shows why it's an epidemic, and proposes a means of continuous correction.

Quicksilver's recommendations revolve around this simple idea: in the face of challenges, today's leaders must learn to recognize what the moment is calling for. To do that we almost always need the perspectives of others. Once you understand the neurobiology of this, and embrace a set of personal practices for dealing with it (like those laid out in this book), you are prepared to lead yourself and others toward the infinite possibilities of what Dr. Michael O'Brien calls the "generative truth." The generative truth is very different from anything you can discover alone.

Here's a small example of how this has worked for me.

At a recent board meeting, one of my directors spoke out forcefully against a controversial decision. The other directors and I agreed the decision was necessary, painful though it might be. This one noisy director, however, wanted to keep talking about all the upset we were going to cause. She wouldn't let it go. My natural reaction was irritation. That irritation was familiar to me. Somehow I've managed to attract irritating board members throughout my thirty-five-year executive career.

As it happened, Michael was at this meeting in his capacity as my executive coach.

"It was so wonderful that she did that," he said to me as soon as the meeting ended.

"You gotta be kidding me," I said. "That was wonderful?"

Of course it was, he explained. In her break with the majority, the outspoken director fully disclosed the pain this decision was going to cause certain groups. Our organization was going to have to lead all concerned through this serious disruption or the decision could fail.

That insight instantly ended my irritation about the affair. As *Quicksilver* explains, the ability to quickly end personal frustration is an essential skill for all leaders. Now, I was no longer dealing with an obstreperous board member. Instead, I was being given a gift that I very much needed. In that instant, my world, and the world I am charged as a leader to help create, changed for the better.

I consider this book a gift that all of us need. I commend it to you, to those you lead, and to those whom you care about.

Still, I must end with a caveat. *Quicksilver* is like a nutrition book. You can't benefit from just reading about healthy food. You have to eat it. I can tell you from personal experience that the "food" in this book is very nutritious.

— MICHAEL D. CONNELLY, M.A., J.D., FACHE
Former CEO
Mercy Health

INTRODUCTION

Invitation to the Reinventors' Ball

By Larry Shook

QUICKSILVER WAS THE NICKNAME given to liquid metal mercury, the shiny stuff used in old-fashioned thermometers. Quicksilver became a metaphor for suddenness and unpredictability. If you ever saw mercury skitter across the floor from a broken thermometer, you know why.

The quicksilver in this book's title refers to two aspects of our world, two sides of the same coin.

One face of that coin seems alarmingly unstable. There you find the unprecedented pace of change of modern life.

Opposite, however, is a scene of almost blindingly bright hopefulness. There you glimpse the infinite ability of the human brain to both respond to change and create change.

One obvious cause of the disorienting change now blurring around us is the basic machine of our times, the computer. Its heart is the microchip. According to Moore's Law, the microchip doubles in power about every eighteen months. Imagine that happening to every other machine in your life—your toaster, your car, the reading light on your nightstand. Year after year. Decade after decade. It wouldn't be long before your toaster would be a nuclear reactor; your car a rocket; your reading light a little sun incinerating anything within millions of miles.

Computers may not be quite that destabilizing, but they're not far from it.

Item: According to Pennsylvania Congressman Paul Kanjorski, chairman of the House Capital Markets Subcommittee, at about eleven o'clock one morning in mid-September 2008, the Federal Reserve Board detected a massive electronic drain of U.S. money market accounts.

Here was something new under the sun: a hidden assault on the spinal cord of the economy. The assault, however, was mounted by consumers, not terrorists. No queue of panicked depositors circled any building. Instead, there was a run on the banks that was perfectly invisible—except to those keeping watch over electrons.

In an hour or two, Kanjorski told the audience of a CSPAN program, some $550 billion was withdrawn. The Fed pumped in $150 billion, but it couldn't stop the bleeding. The nation's central bank announced a $250,000 guarantee per deposit and closed the money market accounts. If it hadn't done that, said Kanjorski, the Fed estimated that by two that afternoon, $5.5 trillion would have disappeared from the banking system.

Citing the conclusions of Federal Reserve Board officials, Kanjorski said that the global economy would have collapsed within 24 hours. Political systems as we know them would have ceased to exist.

That's the scary side of the quicksilver coin, the side that resembles the storyline of a James Bond movie. It has an infinite range of less apocalyptic but no less... *interesting* manifestations.

Item: During a nightclub act, Michael Richards vents a racial tirade. An audience member records it with a cell phone. Thanks to YouTube, in a matter of hours the career of one of America's most brilliant and beloved comedians lies in ruins.

Item: Passengers observe United Airlines baggage handlers throwing guitar cases at Chicago's O'Hare Airport. One of the instruments' owners, Canadian singer and songwriter Dave Carroll, looks on in "terror," as he later immortalizes the incident in lyrics. He alerts United personnel, who respond with indifference. The entertainer spends nine months in a futile effort to get United to compensate him for a broken $3,500 Taylor guitar. Finally, he commemorates the incident in a catchy, lighthearted YouTube video called "United Breaks Guitars." It goes viral, and in no time millions of viewers are tapping their feet to this lampoonery of United's corporate culture.

Little wonder that the lifecycles of products and companies grow shorter and shorter as the latest killer app pulls the rug out from under them. Little wonder that jobs, and whole industries, come and go now with such disconcerting speed. It's part of the rapidly changing portrait of our quicksilver age.

On the other side of the coin is where you find hopeful news from the world of neuroscience. Research shows that the human brain possesses about a hundred billion neurons, connected by about a hundred trillion synapses. These are living cells that think. They think automatically, often based on lessons learned by long-dead ancestors. Clearly, some of those lessons go out of date. On the other hand, our neural heritage lets us think on purpose. Thinking on purpose enables continuous *intentional* learning.

Just how great is our learning potential?

Scientists tell us that the number of potential interactions among our thinking cells—our neurons and synapses—exceeds the number of molecules in the known universe. Here, then, is a galaxy of latent cognitive potential between our ears.

Were we to succeed in focusing the brain's power on the challenges of the "energy crisis," the "food crisis," the inconvenient truth of your choice, evidence is strong that the problems would be quickly solved.

Unfortunately, we're not doing that. In fact, the evidence is just plain disturbing that humanity today suffers from a learning disorder that threatens its survival.

This book offers a solution.

Quicksilver is based on more than twenty-five years of the experience of Dr. Michael O'Brien as an executive coach. He and his team have about a hundred years of executive coaching experience among them. That's a lot of time spent in a rarified, high-judgment environment where individuals are constantly called upon to make decisions that affect countless thousands of lives.

Based on all that experience, Michael and his colleagues have come to a simple conclusion: the most important challenge facing leaders today—and the rest of us, too—is consciousness.

But what does that mean? What it does *not* mean, as Michael uses the term, is idle contemplation of the meaning of life. It means, instead, continuous awareness—sometimes with laser focus—of the unique way each of us sees events and then decides what they mean; decides what, if any, action to take.

Consciousness, as the term is used here, means learning to think differently, on purpose, when we need to. Neuroscience, the hopeful side of the quicksilver coin, reveals that we are capable of doing this, and that the results are transformative. It also shows why thinking differently on purpose is so hard.

This book offers a way to overcome that difficulty. It contains exercises Michael has developed that have proven to be revolutionary, exercises that allow people to shift their perspectives on the fly, in the face of trying circumstances. This instantly changes their experience of events, exposing new, otherwise hidden options. Not coincidentally, the exercises also reprogram the brain, creating new neural/synaptic combinations. That actually changes the world. In a sense, it *creates* the world we live in. This mysterious molecular event may be the seminal phenomenon of great leadership.

Year after year, Michael is invited to teach these exercises to organizations as diverse as the IRS, New York Life, and Procter & Gamble for a simple reason: they work. You cannot perform these practices without changing your life. Learning to constantly perform them in the face of challenge will give you a control over events that is not otherwise possible.

If you are a leader, the practices outlined in this book will lever your natural abilities and constantly help you develop new capacity. This will inspire others to follow your example. While the exercises are deceptively simple, integrating them into your life takes discipline and commitment.

A note: Michael asked me to use my journalism background to help him frame this book's content. The book's ideas flow from Michael's education and experience. The ideas are his. The voice is his, to the best of my ability to translate it. My attempts to do so are based on several years of discussion, an earlier book we wrote together, and a week of intensive tape-recorded interviewing on an island off the Florida coast with ospreys mewling outside above the peaceful spring surf of the Gulf. I am honored and grateful to have been able to make a modest contribution to this book. I truly believe that its subject—consciousness—represents the most important item on the human agenda today.

I think these times welcome all of us to a kind of great ball—a reinventors' ball. Whether you lead only your own life—your infinitely precious life—or the precious lives of many others, I hope you will consider *Quicksilver* to be your personal invitation to the ball. May you choose to dance your heart out.

CHAPTER ONE

WALL STREET'S MONSTER

The Wages of Unconscious Leadership

≈⌣

"Our inferential machinery is not made
for a complicated environment."
—NASSIM NICHOLAS TALEB

IT TURNS OUT THE WORLD really is flat. At least, according to the Flat Earth Society it is. No relic of antiquity, the Society is as much with us as the Federal Reserve Board. You can go to the Web sites of both organizations and check them out.

"Deprogramming the masses since 1547" is the motto of the former.

Motto of the latter: "The Federal Reserve, the central bank of the United States, provides the nation with a safe, flexible, and stable monetary and financial system."

Members of the Flat Earth Society subscribe to a scientific theory that was largely discredited at the time of Aristotle, about 2,300 years ago. Nevertheless, its contemporary adherents cite incontrovertible evidence that the home planet is flat. Evidence to the contrary, they argue—planet portraits snapped from space, say—is a hoax.

Whatever Earth's actual geometrical shape, given its

current financial crisis, public opinion may be divided at the moment over whether the Federal Reserve Board's motto is any more believable than that of the Flat Earth Society.

As an entrée to this book's subject—what leaders need to know about how the working of the human mind governs perceptions, beliefs, and decisions—this is not as ironic as you might think.

Scientists tell us—I trust this is no hoax—that most functions of the brain are unconscious. Even though leaders tend to be better looking, smarter and richer than most of us, it logically follows that they are no more conscious than the rest of us.

The great financial meltdown of 2008 is a textbook example of unconscious leadership if ever there was one.

What would make that deduction untrue, of course, is if leaders took special steps to increase their consciousness. The high rate of organizational misadventure does not suggest they do.

This is upsetting. It conjures an unsettling image—if not exactly of the blind leading the blind, at least of the somnambulant leading the somnambulant. It's enough to make it hard to get a good night's rest.

The great financial meltdown of 2008 that shook the global (or table-shaped) economy to its very foundation is a case in point, a textbook example of unconscious leadership if ever there was one.

After the domino-like collapses of Bear Stearns, Fannie Mae and Freddie Mac, Lehman Brothers, Merrill Lynch, Washington Mutual, insurance giant AIG, international financial services behemoth UBS, and the precipitous tumble of global stock markets, the U.S. Congress passed a $700 billion economic bailout plan, one of the most controversial acts in U.S. history. That was in October 2008. The next month, the Federal Reserve Board proposed an additional $800 billion stimulus package to shore up housing and credit markets. Together these added up to $1.5 trillion, or about $5,000 for every man, woman and child in the country.

It hardly needs saying that for U.S. citizens this was the worst financial quarter in history. It was as though the country had been invaded by a foreign power with completely different economic ideas than ours. What happened?

> It was as though the country had been invaded by a foreign power with completely different economic ideas than ours.

The New York Times, the nation's newspaper of record, published a story suggesting—visually at least—that the cause of our trouble was a crocodile attack.

Its March 23, 2008 story "What Created This Monster?" was accompanied by an illustration of a distinguished suit-clad gentleman—presumably a Wall Street native—reading a newspaper as he perched unsuspectingly on a giant crocodile's snout. "Yes, the Markets Can Bite Back" was the subhead.

The "monster" was an investment product known as a derivative, an asset that has no value itself. (It *derives* its value from something else that does have inherent value—your home mortgage, for instance.)

Historians will probably write that the *Times* story was unfair to crocodiles. Because Wall Street's Monster was created by the leaders of the free world (who were then shocked by its attack), Frankenstein would seem the better poster beast.

So far as I know, the leaders of the free world—members of Congress, federal regulators, Wall Street executives—do not belong to the Flat Earth Society. To the best of my knowledge, they do not believe that the scientific method has been appropriated as a tool of mass deception by some camarilla.

Nevertheless, our present economic chaos suggests that they must have been drunk on their own punch. How else could they have led us into this mess? The thinking and public statements of one man in particular—he was known variously as the Oracle and Maestro—underscores this impression. This is Alan Greenspan, Chairman of the Federal Reserve from 1987 to 2006.

Greenspan's performance offers a powerful example of why leadership is so important to all of us. It's also a priceless exhibit of why, in today's world, *how* leaders think matters more than *what* they think.

Alan Greenspan is demonstrably one of the most accomplished economists of his generation. Under his leadership, there was "no other period of comparable length in which the Federal Reserve System has performed so well," Milton Friedman opined in *The Wall Street Journal* in 2006.

Soon after Greenspan retired, the global economy tumbled into chaos. "We are in the midst of a global crisis that will unquestionably rank as the most virulent since the 1930s," Greenspan himself wrote in the March 11, 2009 *Wall Street Journal*.

Had this time of historic trouble befallen us because

Greenspan's successor, Ben Bernanke, was so much less skilled? Or was it because, as Greenspan wrote in the *Journal*, "the levels of complexity" in today's economy "were too much for even the most sophisticated market players to handle properly and prudently"?

The dizzying events of the meltdown clearly suggest the latter. But is even that true? *Have* we created a world that is too complex for us to manage?

In trying to deconstruct a disaster—an airplane crash, a financial crash—focusing on what decisions were made usually yields a list of "mistakes." From such evidence we typically revise procedures in the faith that different procedures will prevent the mistakes' repetition. (If you don't want history to repeat itself, don't keep doing the same thing.)

> The illusion is that by simply inventorying mistakes we can learn from them and avoid repeating them.

But such evidence of "correctable mistakes," I believe, contains an increasingly dangerous illusion. The illusion is that by simply inventorying mistakes we can learn from them and avoid repeating them. While that may work well enough with sports and aviation, with their comparatively static contexts, it has never been an adequate way of dealing with life itself. This is especially true in the life of a vibrant capitalist economy where the "creative destruction" of healthy competition continuously changes the marketplace and the rules for negotiating it. If the dynamics of human affairs and the flux of the marketplace have always made it true that "things aren't always what they seem to be," never has that been more true than today.

As we'll see in the next chapter, the accelerating new-ness of the digital world ensures this. At an increasing pace, Moore's Law erases the relevance of correcting yesterday's mistakes to solving today's challenges, to say nothing of deal-ing with tomorrow. Moore's Law has turned the economy into a kind of *über* video game, where the landscape and the way things work are continuously unfamiliar. What is needed in such an environment is not a mastery of rules that fit past circumstances but the ability to read change, the ability to maintain a kind of fluid mental hologram of what's going on around you. That's why continuous evaluation of the validity of one's beliefs and perceptions, and recalibration of them as needed, has become so important. As Wall Street's Monster shows, we're not in Kansas anymore.

Most of the reporting I've seen about Wall Street's Monster so far—I'm going to call it that, even though Wall Street didn't create it by itself—has missed this point. The reporting has focused on what decisions were made by what individuals and what subsequently happened. Within journalism's para-digm, some of this reporting has been downright masterly. A good example is "Anatomy of A Meltdown," a recitation of events by John Cassidy in the December 1, 2008 *New Yorker* that was so painstaking as to resemble the slow motion film of a train wreck.

Cassidy's story also captured the bizarre video game-like wilderness where nothing seems to make sense, and through which the economy's fatigued leaders now find themselves wandering.

Of Fed Chairman Bernanke, Cassidy wrote: " 'A lot can still go wrong, but at least I can see a path that will bring us out of this entire episode relatively intact,' he told a visitor to his office in August [2008]."

Within two weeks, Bernanke's world (ours, too, of course) started to fall apart. In one forty-eight-hour period the Dow Jones Industrial Average dropped four hundred points. A few weeks later, between October 6th and October 10th, there was another sickening dive. Nearly a fifth of the wealth reflected in the Dow's index disappeared, the worst loss in a century.

Not surprisingly, the media's replay of these events has led to finger-pointing.

"25 People To Blame For the Economic Mess We're In," trumpeted a cover line of the February 23, 2009 issue of *Time* magazine. Inside was a story about the alleged perpetrators. Accompanying the story was a graphic portraying the perps in a police lineup. Perp No. 3: Alan Greenspan. "He was the one person who could have stopped it," pronounced *Time's* prosecutors.

> I think the mistakes that created Wall Street's Monster were made by dangerously normal people—just like me, just like you.

"About the list," wrote the editors. "The venting of spleen is not a science—it's a joy."

Ahem. Obviously, the problem with this kind of gleeful faultfinding is that it suggests mistakes were made by dangerously stupid, or foolish, or incompetent, or irresponsible people. For the most part, I don't think that's what happened. I think the mistakes that created Wall Street's Monster were made by dangerously normal people—just like me, just like you. I believe that until this is understood, the mistakes will continue with ever more devastating results. I don't have to venture very far out on a limb in saying that. It's already happening.

If someone as demonstrably brilliant, well-educated, and dedicated as Alan Greenspan can make the kind of mistakes the facts now prove that he made, we should all ask why.

What follows is also a kind of anatomy of the meltdown—of Wall Street's Monster—but it has a different perspective from that of John Cassidy's meticulous account.

"We can't retreat to the nineteenth century," the English novelist Ian McEwan recently told an interviewer. "We now have a narrative of self-awareness that we can never escape."

The sequence of events leading up to the financial crisis doesn't suggest that anything like a narrative of self-awareness was operating, at least not one that came close to being equal to the task at hand. On the contrary, certain developments that brought about this crisis are now so obvious as to suggest something more akin to a Big Sleep on the part of leaders.

It's that Big Sleep, and what to do about it, that is the concern of this book.

If someone as demonstrably brilliant, well-educated, and dedicated as Alan Greenspan can make the kind of mistakes the facts now prove that he made, we should all ask why.

The financial world entered a period of radical change beginning in the 1960s, Roger Lowenstein points out in *When Genius Failed*, his fine book about the 1998 wreck of the hedge fund Long-Term Capital Management. A series of events—rampant inflation, the unfixing of the price of gold, the historic bankruptcy of Penn Central Railroad—turned bond trading, a "dull sport" until then, upside down.

"The world of fixed relationships was dead," concludes Lowenstein.

"By the end of the 1970s, firms such as Salomon [Brothers] were slicing and dicing bonds in ways… never dreamed of: blending mortgages together, for instance, and distilling them into bite-sized, easily chewable securities."

A new type of player had entered the game of finance. Wall Street firms were hiring Ph.D. physicists and mathematicians to serve as quantitative financial analysts. These "quants," as they're called, designed exotic new abstractions of derivatives—prodigious arabesques of advanced mathematics—so complicated that only a handful of financial types could understand them.

The world of finance had radically changed. It now seems, however, that no one paid much attention. As a result, a dangerous illusion, the notion that old ways of conducting business still made sense, had dawned.

Led by Harvard's Robert C. Merton, the quants who migrated from academia to Wall Street would "transform finance into a mathematical discipline," as Lowenstein puts it.

The professors put forth complex math models, like the famous Black-Scholes formula. These elegant equations proposed the existence of a clockwork mechanism uniting the physical and psychological variables of the economy.

Belief in that mechanism's verdict on the values of financial securities, coupled with the advent of new computing technology, drove a historic—but fleeting—period of wealth creation in the world's bourses.

"Soon Texas Instruments was advertising in *The Wall Street Journal*, 'Now you can find the Black-Scholes value using our calculator,' " wrote Lowenstein. "This was the true beginning of the derivatives revolution. Never before had professors made such an impact on Wall Street."

Traders also wielded another powerful new tool, computers, which they consulted instead of a thick blue book to see what a security was momentarily trading at. The brave new world of "continuous time finance" had arrived.

Among the results was that the practice of arbitrage, an esoteric form of trading that exploits price differences between markets, exploded.

Arbitrage was now yielding huge profits and astronomical salaries. In 1989, for instance, Salomon Brothers arbitrageur Lawrence Hilibrand took home $23 million. By the early 1990s, writes Lowenstein, arbitrage was supplying most of the venerable banking firm's earnings. How this was happening no one seemed to know.

Lowenstein: "Even investors who had an inkling of *what* Arbitrage [Salomon's department by that name] had earned had no understanding of *how* it had earned it. The nuts and bolts—the models, the spreads, the exotic derivatives—were too obscure."

In retrospect, this can be seen as a flashing light of unconsciousness, a clear warning that new financial understanding, and new leadership, was desperately needed. Wealth was exploding, but the most sophisticated financiers in the world couldn't explain why. It was as though scientists had built the atomic bomb without grasping its physics, much less its implications.

In the 2009 spring of the world's discontent, with crazy weather patterns and the economy in a howling freefall unlike anything ever seen, it was hard to believe that we walked by the warning signs with barely a nod. But we did. What is more troubling still is that even now there is little indication that we have grasped the way our lives have changed. Maybe the simplest way to put it is that our minds are changing the world, but we still aren't changing our minds to match the world we're creating.

In retrospect, this can be seen as a flashing light of unconsciousness, a clear warning that new financial understanding, and new leadership, was desperately needed.

A spectacular episode of economic turbulence a quarter century ago exposed this continuing mismatch. It also showed just how conditional and fragile "wealth" has become in the world we're creating.

"In the summer of 1982, large American banks lost close to all their past earnings (cumulatively), about everything they ever made in the history of American banking—everything," writes former Wall Street trader Nassim Nicholas Taleb in his book *The Black Swan*.

The widely reported proximate cause of that particular bust was the simultaneous default on huge loans by South and Central American countries. Taleb doesn't buy that explanation. The bad loans wouldn't have been made, he argues, but for the bad thinking that led to them. The bad loan products were simply yields of bad thought products.

The thought products were "bad," I would say, because they bore the clear mark of insufficient consciousness.

"All that while [when the banks were handing out their depositors' money] the bankers led everyone, especially themselves, into believing that they were 'conservative,'" continues Taleb. "They are not conservative; just phenomenally skilled at self-deception…"

Taleb continues: "In fact, the travesty repeated itself a decade later, with the 'risk-conscious' large banks once again under financial strain, many of them near-bankrupt, after the real estate collapse of the early 1990s in which the now defunct savings and loan industry required a taxpayer-funded bailout of more than half a trillion dollars. The Federal Reserve bank protected them at our expense: when 'conservative' bankers make profits, they get the benefits; when they are hurt, we pay the costs."

Here was yet another indication that we simply did not understand the world we were creating. Where were these occluding financial storms coming from? For any circumspect observer it seemed as though the economic operating manual used by policymakers was becoming more outdated with each passing year.

Banks needed some new ideas, and the array of lucrative new investment products, the professors' brainchildren, seemed to be a good bet, but not everyone agreed.

Concern about the dangers posed by derivatives dates back at least to the early 1990s, reported *The New York Times* in an October 8, 2008 story, "The Reckoning: Taking Hard New Look at a Greenspan Legacy."

Rep. Edward J. Markey (D-Mass.), chairman of the House subcommittee on telecommunications and finance, tasked the General Accounting Office to study derivatives' risks in 1992.

"Two years later," reported the *Times*, "the office released its report, identifying 'significant gaps and weaknesses' in the regulatory oversight of derivatives.

"'The sudden failure or abrupt withdrawal from trading of any of these large U.S. dealers could cause liquidity problems in the markets and could also pose risks to others, including federally insured banks and the financial system as a whole,' said Charles A. Boshers, head of the GAO, when he testified before Mr. Markey's committee in 1994. 'In some cases intervention has and could result in a financial bailout paid for or guaranteed by taxpayers.'"

Stop the film. From the perspective of this book, here was a golden moment. It was the first of many. Had Wall Street's quants, financial institution leaders, members of the Federal Reserve Board, Senators, Congressmen, the President, their advisors, had a set of *explicit personal practices* that allowed them to proceed more *consciously* in this moment of perfect mystery—perfect *high stakes* mystery—things might have turned out differently. But they didn't. The undetected advance of Wall Street's Monster continued.

Based on his training and experience, the world's most powerful economic policymaker, Fed chairman Greenspan, was not inclined to recommend significant policy adjustments. He simply could not see how the world had changed.

"In his testimony at the time," reported the *Times*, "Mr. Greenspan was reassuring. 'Risks in financial markets, including derivatives markets, are being regulated by private parties,' he said. 'There is nothing involved in federal

> The world's most powerful economic policymaker... could not see how the world had changed.

regulation per se which makes it superior to market regulation."

Still, not even Greenspan was completely asleep to derivatives' significance. "Mr. Greenspan warned that derivatives could amplify crises because they tied together the fortunes of many seemingly independent institutions," reported the *Times*. "'The very efficiency that is involved here means that if a crisis were to occur, that crisis is transmitted at a far faster pace and with some greater virulence,' he said."

But Greenspan managed to disregard his own warning. He "called that possibility 'extremely remote,' adding that 'risk is part of life.'"

In other words, the crisis that ultimately *did* occur, that continues to unfold, Greenspan simply proclaimed to be too unlikely to worry about. The self-correcting forces of the free market, he believed, made the modern economy unsinkable. In a way, Greenspan turned out to be right: the economy proved to be as unsinkable as the Titanic.

In 1997, as the *Times* reported, a powerful federal authority challenged Greenspan's reassurances. This was attorney Brooksley E. Born, chairwoman of the Commodities Futures Trading Commission (CFTC). Born examined the growing risk of derivatives and didn't like what she saw.

Reported the *Times*: "Ms. Born was concerned that unfettered, opaque trading could 'threaten our regulated markets or, indeed, our economy without any federal agency knowing about it,' she said in Congressional testimony. She called for greater disclosure of trades and reserves to cushion against losses."

Born was arguably one of the foremost derivatives experts in the world. She was a distinguished 1964 graduate of Stanford Law School, former president of the Stanford Law Review. She led the derivatives practice of the powerful Washington, D.C. law firm of Arnold & Porter until she became CFTC chairwoman in 1996.

All Born was proposing in 1997, really, was the kind of transparent accounting healthy free markets require, and for investors to be responsible for their own risks.

All Born was proposing in 1997, really, was the kind of transparent accounting healthy free markets require, and for investors to be responsible for their own risks.

How did her governmental colleagues respond?

"Ms. Born's views incited fierce opposition from Mr. Greenspan and Robert E. Rubin, the Treasury secretary then," wrote the *Times*.

Greenspan and Rubin cautioned Born to keep quiet.

"Treasury lawyers concluded that merely discussing new rules threatened the derivatives market. Mr. Greenspan warned that too many rules would damage Wall Street, prompting traders to take their business overseas."

Continued the *Times*: "'Greenspan told Brooksley that she essentially didn't know what she was doing and she'd cause a financial crisis,' said Michael Greenberger, who was a senior director at the Commission. 'Brooksley was this woman who was not playing tennis with these guys and not having lunch with these guys. There was a little bit of the feeling that this woman was not of Wall Street.'"

In early 1998, reported the *Times*, deputy Treasury secretary Lawrence H. Summers "called Ms. Born and chastised her for taking steps he said would lead to a financial crisis...."

Born refused to back down.

"On April 21, 1998," continued the *Times*, "senior federal financial regulators convened in a wood-paneled conference room at the Treasury to discuss Ms. Born's proposal. Mr. Rubin and Mr. Greenspan implored her to reconsider...."

Born refused.

On June 5, 1998, Greenspan, Rubin and Arthur Levitt (Chairman of the SEC), three not-so-wise men, as history would record soon enough, persuaded Congress to disable the stubborn Born "until more senior regulators developed their own recommendations."

Her authority to regulate derivatives was temporarily suspended.

The checking of Brooksley Born, ominous events would signal immediately, would become one of the most fateful developments in modern economic history.

Stop the film again, please. Here was another golden moment. The checking of Brooksley Born, ominous events signaled immediately, would become one of the most fateful developments in recent economic history. Because at this precise juncture, Long-Term Capital Management, a little known hedge fund with significant derivatives exposure, almost collapsed.

LTCM had been founded by a Wall Street star named John Meriwether. Meriwether took a few quants with him when he left Salomon Brothers. LTCM, then, was run by some of the world's best financial minds, two Nobel Prize winners among them. Nevertheless, LTCM's bubble of highly leveraged trading—it had produced returns of over forty percent for several years—finally burst. The only thing that prevented LTCM's self-destruction was something that Greenspan said wasn't supposed to be needed: federal intervention.

In September 1998, the Federal Reserve Bank of New York engineered a $3.6 billion bailout of LTCM by every major Wall Street bank, more than a dozen institutions.

It was a close scrape. Government and industry recognized that the implosion of this one company could have jeopardized global finance.

This, too, was something new under the sun. Like a Himalayan peak at dawn, it threw a giant shadow. The ominous shape now looming on the horizon: massive government bailouts seen as necessary to avert economic Armageddon. Not even a decade had lapsed since the disastrous real estate bust that Taleb wrote of in *The Black Swan*.

The LTCM bailout was a huge sum at the time, and it represented an embarrassing contradiction of Greenspan's assertion that markets could regulate themselves. Nevertheless, $3.6 billion was a molehill compared to what was coming in the form of Wall Street's Monster.

He clung to his belief and rejected data and viewpoints that refuted it.

And still the leaders of the free world were oblivious. Despite this shocking evidence that his faith was unfounded, Greenspan did that little thing that we do. He clung to his belief and rejected data and viewpoints that refuted it.

Federal Reserve Board Chairman Greenspan, SEC

Chairman Arthur Levitt, and Treasury Secretary Rubin were joined at the hip. By now they had clearly succumbed to the toxic strain of groupthink that would soon spawn a hemorrhagic fever of toxic assets that would sweep the world. These three powerful officials advised Congress to permanently shackle the Commodities Futures Trading Commission and Brooksley Born. Congress complied by passing a bill stripping the CFTC of its powers to regulate derivatives.

President Clinton signed the bill.

The official mind was officially closed on the subject of derivatives. A kind of fiscal germ warfare had been unwittingly loosed on the global economy. Nothing now stood between the taxpayers of the world and the wildest gamblers in history. What America's premiere financial institutions were about to do—with the full complicity of the government of the United States—made the high rollers of Monte Carlo and Las Vegas look like senior center bingo players.

> The leaders of the free world committed one of the cardinal errors in tapping humanity's collective genius. They rejected contrary perspectives.

In gagging Brooksley Born and disabling the ability of the CFTC to regulate derivatives' risks, the leaders of the free world committed one of the cardinal errors in tapping humanity's collective genius. They rejected contrary perspectives.

"Diversity and independence are important because the best collective decisions are the product of disagreement and contest, not consensus or compromise," writes James Surowiecki in his superb *The Wisdom of Crowds: Why the Many Are Smarter than the Few and How Collective Wisdom Shapes Business, Economies, Societies, and Nations.*

In removing the perceptions of Born, the General Accounting Office, and the Commodities Futures Trading Commission from the deliberations about how to manage derivatives' dangers, what the leaders of the free world effectively did was disconnect untold billions of neurons and trillions of synapses from the only decision-making apparatus available to manage the problem. Obviously, this wasn't their intention. The result was no less catastrophic for that, however.

Stop the film again. This is a critical moment in the evolution of Wall Street's Monster. It clearly reveals the dynamic of unconsciousness now threatening not just the economy, but civilization itself. It also reveals an irony in the title of Lowenstein's book, *When Genius Failed*. What we have been calling genius can no longer be seen as genius. In today's world, genius without consciousness is not genius at all.

We deal with discrete technological advance almost automatically. Replace an adding machine with an electronic calculator. Replace a typewriter with a computer. The machines themselves teach us how to change in response to the change they bring to our lives.

It's when the consequence of technological change compounds itself that it becomes imponderable. That's when you get conditions that allow a single company most people never heard of to threaten the global economy. It's when you get a commercial ecosystem in which *one trader* of humble background from a village in Brittany (Jérôme Kerviel of Société Générale) can jeopardize the world's economy.

In such an environment, certainty is the foe. There can be

no certainty in the forecast of cause and effect. This is because everything keeps getting more connected to everything else. Everything depends on everything else. Moment by moment the future becomes more purely conditional, more sublimely unpredictable. The ability of the stroke of a butterfly's wing in the Amazon Basin to lead to a tornado in Texas is tenuous by comparison. In a setting like this, ideology is madder than terrorism. And more destructive.

The antidote, the *only* antidote, is a new kind of consciousness.

Brooksley Born, somehow immune to the groupthink afflicting her colleagues, continued with her valiant efforts to wake up everyone about the impending disaster. She publicized the terrifying meaning of Long-Term Capital Management. Namely, that a beast of financial apocalypse had already arrived.

> **Moment by moment the future becomes more purely conditional, more sublimely unpredictable. In a setting like this, ideology is madder than terrorism. And more destructive.**

"Reportedly, LTCM managed to borrow $125 billion, approximately 100 times its capital," Born wrote in a paper she presented to the business law section of the American Bar Association in November 1998.

Remember the date. 1998. Ten years before the Bust of 2008. An entire decade of not learning, not waking up.

Born had flagged something else new under the sun. Commercial banks—Bank of America, Wells Fargo—had traditionally operated at a debt/equity ratio of ten or twelve to one. That is, they had lent only ten times as much money as they had on deposit. Wall Street's investment banks had been allowed to leverage debt of thirty to forty times their equity. But LTCM was a very different beast, Born explained. Based on its borrowing of one hundred times more than its capital, it was then able "to enter into derivatives positions with a notional value of approximately $1.25 trillion—or 1,000 times its capital."

This would be the equivalent of you borrowing $100 million and putting up your $100,000 house as collateral.

How could this possibly be? One reason was that derivatives had won extraordinary accounting status. Thanks in no small part to Wall Street lobbying, their liabilities were allowed to be kept secret. They did not have to be disclosed on the balance sheets of the investment banks that sold them. Their ultimate value, then, was a mystery, shrouded under a kind of official secrets act.

The scope of that mystery beggared the imagination.

According to the *Times*, by the spring of 2008 the global investment in derivatives exceeded a galactic $40 trillion. That equals nearly $6,000 for every man, woman and child on the planet. (Divide $40 trillion by the world population of 6.7 billion.)

The New Yorker magazine saw that estimate and raised it. In a November 10, 2008 article about the crisis, "Melting Into Air," the magazine wrote that "the total trade in derivative products around the world is counted in the hundreds of trillions of dollars. Nobody knows the exact figure, but the notional amount certainly exceeds the total value of all the world's economic output, roughly sixty-six trillion dollars, by a huge factor—perhaps tenfold."

By that accounting, derivatives had indebted every resident of Earth to the tune of roughly $98,000. It was the fiscal equivalent of Ebola virus escaping species containment. Here was a rampage toward some new equilibrium that would be unknowable until it was achieved.

The threat was Biblical. No wonder Jesus was fond of parables.

"Therefore I speak to them in parables," he says in Matthew 13:13, *"because they seeing see not; and hearing they hear not, neither do they understand."*

Indeed. Among those who did not understand derivatives, as he admitted to the *Times*, was Princeton economics professor Alan S. Blinder, holder of a Ph.D. in economics from M.I.T., former vice chairman of the Federal Reserve Board. Billionaire investor George Soros said he avoided derivatives, because he didn't understand them, either. Gulp.

Derivatives had created a debt bomb that seemed more related to nuclear physics than finance. Theoretically, the only limit on the power of a nuclear weapon, their designers have long noted, is the capacity of a mass to absorb the blast.

Little wonder two of the world's foremost investors invoked the image of nuclear Armageddon in trying to put their understanding of derivatives into words.

Felix Rohatyn, the investment banker famous for saving New York City from bankruptcy in the 1970s, called derivatives potential "hydrogen bombs."

Warren Buffett, the man widely regarded as the world's greatest stock market investor, in the 2002 Berkshire Hathaway annual report famously called derivatives "weapons of financial mass destruction." Buffet wrote that he and Berkshire Hathaway vice chairman Charles T. Munger were "of one mind in how we feel about derivatives and the trading activities that go with them. We view them as time bombs, both for the parties that deal in them and the economic system…"

> Derivatives had created a debt bomb that seemed more related to nuclear physics than finance.

Even as the fear and trembling over derivatives grew, Greenspan remained sanguine. In 2004 he told Congress: "Not only have individual financial institutions become less vulnerable to shocks from underlying risk factors, but also the financial system as a whole has become more resilient."

History can be so cruel.

In March 2008, the nation was stunned by the $30 billion federal bailout of Bear Stearns. This was an order of magnitude worse than the disaster of Long-Term Capital Management of the previous decade. Here was a new kind of stock market index, a measure of the cost of unconsciousness.

Now economists were bracing for the worst. Because of the modern world's extreme interconnectedness, explained *The New York Times* in a piece titled, "A Wall St. Domino Theory," experts feared "that one failure could spread across the financial system."

By this time the unconsciousness embedded in the management of derivatives was undeniable. Wall Street's Monster wasn't just slouching toward Manhattan. It was thundering down upon it. The ground was shaking; the windows were rattling; coffee mugs skittered across desks.

By October 2008, what Greenspan had seen as the unthinkable had happened: the global financial system lay in ruins. Central bankers the world over had put their economies on life support with massive infusions of public money. The world held its breath to see if their efforts would succeed.

Those charged with protecting the world against this rough beast, this monster of their own creation, couldn't believe what had happened.

Greenspan testified before Congress on October 23, 2008 that he was in "shocked disbelief" that bankers had failed to protect their own system, as he had entrusted them to do. He saw the resulting global economic crisis as a "once-in-a-lifetime credit tsunami."

Never mind that the GAO and CFTC had pointed to the tsunami rushing toward the beach a decade earlier. Maestro Greenspan, Wall Street, and the U.S. government just didn't seem able to get their minds around how much the world had changed while they were sleeping.

Greenspan's admission would seem ridiculously naïve were it not for the schizophrenia of humanity's technological virtuosity/imbecility reflected in the sinking of the Titanic, World War I, nuclear arms, NASA space shuttle disasters—and now Wall Street's Monster. It is just that inconsistency that mandates a practice of consciousness like the one advocated in this book.

Based on my experience coaching executives in the techniques of this book's exercises, I have no doubt that our present crisis would have been averted had a critical mass of key decision-makers been engaged in such a practice. I also have no doubt that our problems can only get worse until we take the appropriate steps of waking ourselves up.

The map of the world installed in our brains by our education and experience of yesterday's world does not depict the terrain in which we now find ourselves. It's just that simple. The only way to proceed in today's world is with humility and intense, constant curiosity. We need to leave the massive query engine between our ears in a constant search mode.

When the false universe of derivative values fell into chaos, unleashing Wall Street's Monster, it was instantly clear that the math models had been wrong. They did not portray the physical world after all. They merely projected a magic lantern show, an illusion, from the mathematicians' minds.

But where did the illusion come from? Was it the result of poor decisions made by leaders who simply lacked the intelligence, training, or experience to know better? Or was the cause more… "organic?"

In *The Black Swan*, Taleb makes an observation that argues for the latter.

> The only way to proceed in today's world is with humility and intense, constant curiosity.

"Our inferential machinery is not made for a complicated environment," he writes. "Consider that in a primitive environment there is no consequential difference between the statements *most killers are wild animals* and *most wild animals are killers*. There is an error here, but it is almost inconsequential. Our statistical intuitions have not evolved for a habitat in which these subtleties can make a big difference."

From my perspective as an educator and consultant, I consider that a misdiagnosis. I don't think the problem is our inferential machinery. I think the problem is the way we're using it.

Obviously, there's a way to use the brain that yields the impression that the world is flat. Just as clearly, you can use it to reach the conclusion that running up a $1.25 trillion exposure in derivatives debt really doesn't matter.

Clearly, both conclusions matter a great deal—if, that is, you prefer not to confuse the Earth with an ironing board. Or blow up its economy into very little pieces.

The 2008 meltdown is undoubtedly one of the most significant events in economic history. Scholars will study it for decades. For the purposes of this book, however, Greenspan's March 2009 *Wall Street Journal* commentary is a suitable enough postscript. The headline, "The Fed Didn't Cause the Housing Bubble," captured its exculpatory spirit.

The culprit, Greenspan argued, was not the federal-funds rate in the U.S., but a global decline in long-term interest rates owing to the dynamics of a global economy. He didn't even mention the virus of toxic assets for which he and his colleagues bore direct responsibility.

"The solutions for the financial-market failures revealed by the crisis are higher capital requirements and wider prosecution of fraud—not increased micromanagement by government entities," he wrote.

Higher capital requirements, of course, is one of the

solutions Brooksley Born had been advocating when Team Greenspan silenced her. Disclosure of the actual asset values of derivatives was the other. The latter would have been a kind of sunlight capable of disinfecting much of the fraud and untenable speculation surrounding derivatives that now has the global economy on life support. In effect, the massive bailouts now keeping the economy afloat put taxpayers in the position of involuntarily subsidizing both gambling and crime. These are the wages of unconsciousness.

For Greenspan to still see what Born, the GAO, Buffett, Soros, Rohatyn and others were saying about derivatives as an advocacy of government micromanagement is a little like seeing belief in the need for stop signs as an attempt to micromanage drivers.

The point is that Greenspan still appears to believe that it was a tsunami, not unconsciousness, that swamped our world. His delusive stubbornness is a caution for all of us. We are all biologically disposed to believe that we can comprehend the road ahead based on the one just traveled. This, I believe, is the inferential hazard to which Taleb refers. I agree it is a very serious hazard. I disagree that it is unmanageable.

Three days after Greenspan's *Wall Street Journal* op-ed piece, the paper ran another commentary offering a poignant refrain about the nation's "pandemic of fear." It was by the graceful Peggy Noonan. Headline: "There's No Pill for This Kind of Depression."

Noonan noted a variety of bleak indicators. Anti-depressant drug sales are robust, gun sales soar, people are withdrawing cash from the bank and demanding more gold coins than supply can match.

"Five weeks ago, when I asked a Titan on Wall Street what one should do to be safe in the future, he took me aback with the concreteness of his advice, and its bottom-line nature," she wrote. "Everyone should try to own a house, he said, no matter how big or small, but it has to have some land, on which you should learn how to grow things."

We are all biologically disposed to believe that we can comprehend the road ahead based on the one just traveled.

This evidence of fear driving people to ground was underscored by another anecdote. It was of one of Noonan's friends surfing Internet real estate ads, hunting for a rural place to hide.

"I asked if she had a picture in her head of what she was looking for," wrote Noonan, "and she joked that she wanted to go where Atticus Finch made his summation to the jury. I don't think it was really a joke. She's not looking for a new place, she's looking for the old days."

The impulse to run away is irrational, of course. There is no "away." Besides, as the old saying has it, "wherever we go, there we are."

To me the evidence is overwhelming that our best hope lies in learning to tap the mystical genius we share that Surowiecki writes about in *The Wisdom of Crowds*. In citing feats of combined wisdom that seem downright magical—the ability of a group to guess the dressed weight of an ox with uncanny precision, or to pinpoint the location of a drowned submarine to within a few yards—Surowiecki convincingly makes the case that "the crowd is holding a nearly complete picture of the world in the collective brain... You could say it's as if we've been programmed to be collectively smart."

If that is true (and my experience persuades me it is), what we really need is not drugs, guns and bullion, or a place to hole up, but consciousness. We need a practice for methodically tapping our shared genius with its infinite horizon of possibility. With apologies to FDR, I would say that the only thing we have to fear is the unconsciousness that deprives us of our birthright.

> We need a practice for methodically tapping our shared genius with its infinite horizon of possibility.

Noonan writes that people are afraid now that we have lost a way of life that we cannot retrieve. If that way of life is the unconsciousness that brought us Wall Street's Monster, I say good riddance. If that world is dead, I propose a toast worthy of a royal hope: The world is dead. Long live the world.

CHAPTER TWO

THE WAY WE ARE

The Wages of Unconscious Leadership

Unable to differentiate between physical and psychological stress, the brain has developed a genius for denial and an aptitude for "cognitive static."

*"All I can say is, beware of geeks...
bearing formulas."*
—WARREN BUFFET

IN THE MID-1960s, an American Air Force colonel named Ed Orr had an experience while he was stationed in Turkey that would haunt him all his life.

Orr's job required him to travel to remote military outposts over the first modern Turkish highways. The routes covered vast emptiness, and except for the rare semi truck hauling freight, Orr's was often the only vehicle on the road.

The highlight of Orr's travels was the occasional sight of a lone shepherd with a huge flock of sheep, slowly crossing the plain along an ancient caravan route. The herds contained a thousand sheep and more. They were always flanked by a pair of enormous livestock guardian dogs. It was a scene right out of the Bible. Orr always pulled over to drink it in.

Orr was troubled by how frequently he came across the

bodies of the huge dogs lying beside the road. It made no sense. There was so little traffic on the roads, and the flocks always seemed far enough away that Orr couldn't understand how the dogs were getting hit. Until he saw it happen.

He was pulled over one day marveling at the sepia tableau of a shepherd, his sheep and dogs, when a semi appeared on the horizon. One of the dogs slowly separated itself from the flock and ambled toward the road. After a few moments, the dog gave a mild bark. The truck kept coming. The dog barked louder. The truck continued. The dog loped toward the road, intensifying its warnings as the truck bore down.

Soon the dog stood on the shoulder, barking ferociously. No living creature on two legs or four could have ignored the enormous dog's threat. As the truck roared by at high speed, the dog attacked, flinging itself into the grill.

Orr was in a state of shock.

Why…?

And then it dawned on him.

The dog came from a world in which there were no trucks. There were, however, bears, wolves, jackals, and other predators. To the dog, the truck was a dangerous intruder.

Orr's experience is a powerful metaphor for the shock of the new. Its symmetry with the arrival of hand-held calculators, computers and quants on Wall Street at about the same time is at least interesting.

As this book was being completed, it was clear that the impact of the semi truck on the Anatolian Plateau was trivial compared to the global impact of Wall Street's Monster. For months, the media rang with daily accounts of the rampage.

Every developed economy in the world was impacted, perhaps transformed. The world's central bankers scrambled with massive infusions of public money to keep not just economies but nations, civilization itself, intact. It was too late to put the monster back in its cage, but there was no shortage of pundits pointing out what had created the monster in the first place.

A November 8, 2008 *Wall Street Journal* article quoted something Warren Buffett said during an interview with PBS's Charlie Rose: "All I can say is, beware of geeks...bearing formulas." The same issue quoted Harry Markowitz, the "father of portfolio theory," saying, "Selling people what sellers and buyers don't understand is not a good thing."

Perhaps not. But how we understand anything is no simple matter.

Brain researchers tell us that the way we perceive the world is determined by neural networks inside our brain. Those networks control what we think, feel and do. That means we can think, feel and do nothing for which we do not have the neural structures.

The sublime human irony, one brought into empirical focus by neuroscience only in the decade or so before the appearance of Wall Street's Monster, is this: our experience of the world creates neural structures that add to and alter our genetic inheritance. Those neural structures are the blueprint of our lives. They dictate our understanding of the world. They govern our response to events.

> We can think, feel and do nothing for which we do not have the neural structures.

Because of this, our actions do not always follow

logically from the external stimuli that trigger them. Trigger. Remember that word. You're going to be tested on it for the rest of your life.

The point about triggers is that they are uniquely our own. The world is its own place. Our triggered responses to it are as unique to us as our fingerprints.

The external world, which is forever new, triggers our internal world—this neurological reliquary, this synaptic remembrance of things past—which is forever old. Older, in any event, than this moment, and the next…

The label science gives this behavioral echo chamber is "structural determinism." Structural determinism is a five-dollar label with a ten-cent meaning.

What it means, if you are an ancient breed of livestock guardian dog, for instance, is that the first day a Mack truck hurtles into your world may be your last. Never mind that your kind has had a long and glorious run. Never mind that your noble ancestors are immortalized in ancient Sumerian bas reliefs in recognition for services rendered in guiding humanity from hunting and gathering to pastoralism.

So long and thanks for all the sheep. That was then. The Mack truck is now.

Structural determinism also helps explain why new math and new machines arrived on Wall Street with their implications veiled. The extraordinary disruptions they portended—what Greenspan, one of the world's smartest economists, could only compare to an act of God, a tsunami—had never been experienced before.

(In trying to explain the economic crisis, Congressman Kanjorski also turned to an oceanic metaphor. "Somebody threw us in the middle of the Atlantic Ocean without a life raft, and we're trying to determine what's the closest shore, and whether there's any chance in the world to swim that far. We don't know," he told a CSPAN audience.)

Because the world is always changing, our neural structures can never reflect more than an approximation of it. For most of our history that approximation has been good enough, or else we wouldn't still be here.

The big lesson of Wall Street's Monster, however, and so many of the major challenges now facing us, is that the advance of civilization keeps upping the ante, keeps increasing the spread between what we know and what we need to know. The real arbitrage needed from leaders today has to do with learning how to cope with this differential. The bottom line not just of the economy but also of society itself depends on it.

The good news about Wall Street's Monster is that, among our challenges *du jour*—energy, the threat of epidemics caused by super bugs, pollution, weapons of mass destruction, global warming, etc.—it is tame enough to offer a wonderful dress rehearsal. As Jonathan Lash, president of the World Resources Institute, says: "Nature does not do bailouts."

From my perspective of nearly three decades as an executive coach, it looks to me as though Wall Street's Monster could be a godsend. This is because of Einstein's famous caution:

"Problems cannot be solved by the same level of thinking that created them." While that apothem has won plenty of lip service, humanity still hasn't figured out how to apply it. I think I know why.

Practically speaking, the "level of thinking" that needs to be changed has to do with consciousness. This means learning to become objectively aware, in a timely fashion, of what the mind subjectively produces.

"Where did that idea come from?" "Is it useful?" "Is it accurate?"

That sounds banal. Sages and poets have been saying it forever.

"The unexamined life is not worth living."
—Socrates, 399 B.C.

"We are disturbed not by events,
but by the views that we take of them."
—Epictetus, a few centuries later.

"There is nothing good or bad, but thinking makes it so."
—Shakespeare, *Hamlet*

"The mind is its own place and in itself,
can make a Heaven of Hell, a Hell of Heaven."
—Milton, *Paradise Lost*

By now, most of us are familiar with neuroscience's discoveries, as breathlessly reported in the popular press. It's worth reviewing just a few highlights, however.

The brain has a hundred billion cells, neurons, which are capable of dazzling permutations of synaptic interactions. The conscious portion of the brain makes up seventeen percent of its mass and governs but a tiny fraction—two to four percent—of our perceptions and behaviors. (This seems a plausible explanation for why our quicksilver technology keeps surprising us.) Non-conscious brain tissue, on the other hand, constitutes eighty-three percent of the total, controlling ninety-six percent to ninety-eight percent of our perceptions and actions.

The conscious portion of the brain makes up seventeen percent of its mass and governs but a tiny fraction—two to four percent—of our perceptions and behaviors.

Our environment has been molding the brain from the time hominids emerged. That was five to seven million years ago, archaeologists tell us. It was the genius of the autopilot unconscious brain that allowed us to navigate terra incognita.

The conscious brain serves our will. The non-conscious brain automatically runs our organism, performing such handy services as the ten quadrillion biochemical reactions per second that keep us going.

One of the more fascinating of the countless services performed by the non-conscious brain—one especially important for leaders to understand—is pain management.

In his provocative book *Vital Lies, Simple Truths: The Psychology of Self-Deception*, Daniel Goleman explains that the human genius for denial is biologically based and inseparable from our survival skills. Human beings, notes Dr. Goleman, have pain management systems similar to those of such primitive species as snails and leeches. The common factor: opiate receptors. Their purpose is momentary numbing in order to avoid the distraction of pain. This is handy for all creatures that sometimes need to block pain in order to escape death.

You have seen this mechanism at work if you have ever watched a wildlife program showing a lion pulling down a gazelle. One moment the gazelle is an adrenaline-fueled projectile in the full flight of panic. The next, with the lion's jaws clamped on some part of its anatomy, the prey seems to be in a hypnotic state. The lion's bite has triggered a flush of anesthesia in the gazelle's body. If the gazelle is still capable of wrenching itself free and making another sprint for survival, it will be able to do so without the distraction of pain.

> A mysterious aspect of human pain management is that researchers have not been able to identify how the brain differentiates between the physical and psychological varieties.

Surprisingly, being eaten by a lion apparently doesn't hurt that much. Goleman illustrates with an account by the famous Scottish missionary David Livingston ("Dr. Livingston, I presume?") of surviving a lion attack.

"Growling horribly close to my ear, he shook me as a terrier does a rat," Dr. Livingston wrote. "The shock produced a stupor similar to that which seems to be felt by a mouse after the first shake of the cat. It caused a sort of dreaminess in which there was neither sense of pain nor feeling of terror, though [I was] quite conscious of all that was happening. It was like what patients partially under the influence of chloroform describe, who see the operation but feel not the knife."

A mysterious aspect of human pain management is that researchers have not been able to identify how the brain differentiates between the physical and psychological varieties. At the level of what stress research pioneer Hans Selye called "the first mediator," the brain does not appear to make a distinction.

This is unfortunate for leaders who don't understand (and in my experience, most of them don't) this singular aspect of human nature. Bear markets as well as real bears provoke anxiety. Anxiety, explains Goleman, "is a particular blend of emotion and cognition." This potent mixture of feelings and thought comes in infinite forms, but they're all designed to keep you alive by stirring you to action.

There's good news and bad news about anxiety.

First, the good news. In one sense you don't have to learn how to have anxiety. Mother Nature installed it as a free peripheral. She knows you come into this world clueless, not knowing where, who or what you are, not knowing down which tunnels lie the cheese of life, liberty and happiness. So she arms you with hair-trigger fight or flight anxiety reflexes to help keep actual bears from eating your body, and bear markets from eating your IRA.

Now the bad news. It turns out that you actually *do* have to learn how to manage your anxiety, in the sense that if you don't have it, it will have you.

"While stress arousal is a fitting mode to meet emergency, as an ongoing state, it is a disaster," writes Goleman. Physically, the disaster of chronic anxiety takes the form of a witch's brew of stress-mediated disease. This is because the powerful chemistry of the fight or flight mechanism simply wears out the body if it's left switched on. It can (and does, at epidemic rates) cause heart disease, asthma attacks, even obesity.

The powerful chemistry of the fight or flight mechanism simply wears out the body if it's left switched on.

Psychologically, anxiety causes what Goleman refers to as "cognitive static."

"The essence of anxiety is the intrusion of distress into physical and mental channels that should be clear," writes Goleman. "A nagging worry invades sleep, keeping one awake half the night. A persistent fear imposes itself into one's thoughts, distracting from the business at hand."

Additionally, Goleman explains, anxiety can also trigger an automatic blocking response that causes the anxiety to be hidden from conscious awareness. The result: psychological blind spots that are every bit as real as the physical blind spot created by the way your optic nerves connect your brain to your retina.

Because Goleman was equating a psychological with a physiological phenomenon, he wanted to make sure his readers understood the latter.

"Ordinarily what is missed by the one eye is compensated for by overlapping vision in the other," he wrote. "Thus ordinarily we do not notice our blind spots. But when one eye is closed, the blind spot emerges. To see your blind spot, close your left eye and hold this book at arm's length with your right hand while focusing on the [X]. Very slowly, move the book toward you and back again. Somewhere between ten and fifteen inches away the circle will seem to disappear."

Try this now for yourself.

When the brain numbs anxiety, it creates what Goleman calls "blanks in experience," the self-deception referred to in his book's title. Again, these blanks are automatic, normal, and ubiquitous in the human experience.

That means that at this very moment there are certain blanks in the lives of everyone. Some of those blanks—most of them, probably—are relatively inconsequential. That is, we are well served by the brain's helpful screening of them. Other experiential blanks, however, are ominous, and no modern leader can afford the inability to distinguish between the two.

While there may be many sources of mental anxiety in your life that cause you to consciously reach for the gin or antidepressant, there are many others where the subconscious brain beats you to the punch. Goleman cites such classic examples as family violence, alcoholism, racism.

"In our family there were two very clear rules," Goleman quotes one adult child of an alcoholic. "The first was that there is nothing wrong here, and the second was, don't tell anyone."

Of this hauntingly elusive aspect of the human condition—"how we notice and how we do not notice"—Goleman writes:

"The difficulty is that we have no precise words for it… there are, it seems, vital parts of our lives which are, in a sense, missing—blanks in experience…. That we do not experience them is a fact which we know only vaguely, if at all…."

Goleman borrows the Latin term "lacuna," which means gap or hole, to describe this curious psychic mechanism that banishes events from our conscious awareness.

"Lacunas are psychological analogues of the opioids and their antiattention effects," he writes. "Lacunas are black holes of the mind, diverting attention from select bits of subjective reality—specifically, certain anxiety-evoking information. They operate on attention like a magician misdirecting his audience to look over there, while over here a key prop slips out of sight."

> The intriguing paradox, of course, is that while consciousness itself can trigger anxiety, anxiety can trip us into unconsciousness—without our even knowing.

This is a critical aspect of human nature for leaders to understand in an age that demands new levels of consciousness. The intriguing paradox, of course, is that while consciousness itself can trigger anxiety, anxiety can trip us into unconsciousness—without our even knowing.

"Our failure to experience these aspects of our lives appears due to causes deep within our consciousness," writes Goleman. "It results in an incapacity to bring attention to bear on certain crucial aspects of our reality, leaving a gap in that beam of awareness which defines our world from moment to moment...."

Our blind spots, stresses Goleman, create not just our own reality but social reality, too. Individuals create the reality of families, groups, communities, organizations, nations. Their reality controls investment firms, central banks, government agencies.

"This social reality is pocked with zones of tacitly denied information. The ease with which such social blind spots arise is due to the structure of the individual mind. Their social cost is shared illusions."

Is that why Greenspan and others could not see the derivatives danger that the General Accounting Office and the chairwoman of the Commodities Futures Trading Commission were trying desperately to point out?

Another explanation, of course, is that some of America's most important leaders were dangerously stupid. I don't think that's the case. I think their distinguished careers *prove* it wasn't the case. The more likely scenario is that they were dangerously normal in not noticing what was plainly there to notice.

But whereas Goleman declares that his topic is "how things work, not what to do with them," our purpose is the latter. The social reality for which leaders are responsible, of course, is that of their organizations.

> Noticing how one notices—a supreme act of self-examination— must be considered a core competency of every modern leader.

The premise of this book is that noticing how one notices— a supreme act of self-examination—must be considered a core competency of every modern leader. This isn't just because of the lag between our neural landscape and the external landscape created by our technology. It is also because it is the very business of leaders to continuously lead their organizations into the unknown. And obviously you can't *lead* anyone anywhere without going there first yourself.

That's why it's called leadership, not pushership.

One more thing: the design of our brain sees to it that the unknown provokes anxiety. "You don't know where you are," says the brain in the presence of the unknown. "Pay attention. Be careful."

So leadership makes people nervous, beginning with leaders. The speed of a conscious impulse in the brain: 140 mph, max. The speed of an unconscious impulse: 100,000 mph, plus.

The right neural aid could have helped all concerned loosen the synaptic bonds that hobbled them.

What this means is that if someone warns you, say, that derivatives are financial weapons of mass destruction, your unconscious reaction is going to hit a lot faster than your conscious reaction. Not only that, your unconscious reaction may be so unsettling that your unconscious mind just blots it out before you begin to consciously stew on it.

In a sense, the General Accounting Office and Commodities Futures Trading Commission Chairwoman Brooksley Born were attempting to offer leadership on the hidden dangers of derivatives. What they did not do—and what neuroscience suggests may have doomed their efforts—was offer a "neural aid" to help their audience. The right neural aid could have helped all concerned loosen the synaptic bonds that hobbled them instead of cinching them down.

Keep in mind those synaptic links are the byproduct of *past* experience. Again, their relevance to current circumstances requires evaluation, consciousness. The decision to engage in such ongoing evaluation is obviously a much more structural, and therefore conditional, approach to thought and judgment than we are taught in school.

Derivatives seemed to be a golden egg. Naturally, there was tremendous neuronal resistance to any suggestion to the contrary. What kind of neural aid might have helped Born and the GAO summon group intelligence from the Fed, Wall Street, Congress and the Clinton Administration concerning derivatives?

All Larry and I have to go on in understanding the debate over derivatives that raged during the Clinton years is the subsequent reporting of it. We weren't there. Had I participated as an executive coach I would know details that would let me comment with some precision, but I think I can still make useful general observations.

The first neural aid that would have helped Born and the GAO help their counterparts would have been to follow the fifth Quicksilver Principle. (See the list in the back of the book.) Namely: "Don't resist resistance. What you resist persists."

The reporting suggests that Born and the GAO were deeply worried about derivatives. Who can blame them? It also suggests that their counterparts were just as worried about the dangers of government attempts to regulate derivatives. Who can blame them? Worry is a form of fear. A fear-based position on any subject creates a psychological state of opposition. Psychological opposition is very differ-

When we feel threatened by each other's views, our discussions change. They become oppositional.

ent from just having a different idea about something than someone else. Passionate differences of opinion on all kinds of subjects are common, of course—music, sports, how much ketchup to put on scrambled eggs. On such topics our differences may be deep (*You put ketchup on eggs?!*), but nothing about them scares us. Because of that, we can have spirited, enjoyable, even illuminating conversations about them.

However, when we feel threatened by each other's views, our discussions change. They become oppositional. Oppositional psychology poses a clear and present danger to straight thinking. It tends to trigger synaptic fight-or-flight "snapping." That's why the "large friendly letters" on the cover of *The Hitchhiker's Guide to the Galaxy* offer such good advice. "Don't Panic." It applies whether you're lost in the stars or just don't know what to do about derivatives.

I'm not saying that fear is bad or avoidable. In fact, it's neither. I am saying that it's manageable and that it is in your best interest to manage it. (See Chapter Four.)

Curiosity suspends opposition and kills panic.

When fear is involved in a difference of opinion, as it understandably was in the debate over derivatives, there's a proven way to manage it: *curiosity.* Whenever you feel yourself in passionate opposition with someone, if you can, however momentarily, replace that opposition with passionate curiosity about the opposing view, you will trigger a tiny and profound shift deep within the neuronal circuitry of your brain. Neuroscience calls that shift a "roadblock." It sets you on a different path. Curiosity suspends opposition and kills panic.

The fundamental division between Born and Greenspan contained priceless assets that could have been tapped with potentially transformative results. First, both camps shared a sincere desire to protect and enhance the economy. Second, the brain trust represented in the two camps was almost certainly capable of finding the best solution. Third, their differences were actually their strengths, because they represented the three essential components for tapping group intelligence: diversity; independence; decentralization.

Another neural aid that both camps could have offered each other was to simply own their own stories about their understanding of derivatives' risks. Deeply embracing the conclusion that their views of the situation were nothing more than an artifact resulting from their own life experience would have imbued the discussion with stimulating *humility*. It would have inevitably improved the quality of group decision-making. This may seem like a bromide, but history shows why it isn't.

> Deeply embracing the conclusion that their views of the situation were nothing more than an artifact resulting from their own life experience would have imbued the discussion with stimulating humility.

Think of the Bay of Pigs fiasco. "How could I have been so stupid?" President Kennedy wondered in the immediate aftermath of the failed invasion of Cuba. JFK, a Pulitzer Prize-winning author, led a storied inner circle of "the best and the brightest" into a classic set of blunders immortalized in Irving Janis's seminal book, *Groupthink.*

Long before the Bay of Pigs reflected the macro outlines of groupthink it was preceded by critical micro reality in the neural canyons of the best and the brightest. Had the central players in the Bay of Pigs fiasco and the key players in the derivatives fiasco had explicit personal practices in place like those recommended in this book, a myriad of neural roadblocks would have altered the synaptic events that led to the invasion of Cuba and the "tsunami" that caused our leaders to think that, "Somebody threw us in the middle of the Atlantic Ocean without a life raft."

Still another neural aid both camps could have used was to check and see if they had any stories about each other that prejudiced their views and jeopardized their openness. Wall Street's Monster was preceded by a classic regulatory debate. Because of that, I'd be surprised if unhelpful stories like "this is typical Wall Street greed," and "this is typical bureaucratic meddling in the marketplace" were absent. Owning such stories as a *personal artifact*, not a reflection of "reality," would have been a potentially powerful neural shift. It could easily have led to a cascade of other neural shifts on the part of those trying to make sense of derivatives' dangers. Would that have improved the quality of the group's decision-making? It sure could have.

This is the intimately personal approach to leadership that I think neuroscience's findings now impose on us. It concerns

> Owning such stories as a personal artifact, not a reflection of "reality," would have been a potentially powerful neural shift.

how the world between our ears shapes the world we walk through. I have helped my clients take just this approach and have shared their exhilaration as they found the answers to challenges in the one place such answers can be found: inside themselves.

By revealing how unfathomably limitless human possibility really is, neuroscience has made leadership more exciting, and more hopeful, than ever before in history.

In his book *The Brain That Changes Itself*, Norman Doidge, M.D., refers to what he calls "the neuroplastic revolution." It is a revolution, because it changes our fundamental understanding of what it is to be human.

Neuroplasticity refers to the brain's never-ending creation of new tissue with which to think and learn. Dr. Doidge quotes Dr. Michael Merzenich, "the world's leading researcher on brain plasticity," saying: "The cerebral cortex is actually selectively refining its processing capacities to fit each task at hand."

> The brain is not an inanimate vessel that we fill; rather it is more like a living creature with an appetite, one that can grow and change itself.

The profound implication of that, writes Doidge, is that the brain "doesn't simply learn; it is always 'learning how to learn.' The brain Merzenich describes is not an inanimate vessel that we fill; rather it is more like a living creature with an appetite, one that can grow and change itself with proper nourishment and exercise."

If you want to be all that you can be, in other words, you need to learn how to use your brain properly. Among other things, such findings show why the personal knowledge we rely on, if not constantly evaluated, can soon become the opposite: ignorance. ("It ain't so much what we don't know that gets us into trouble as what we do know that ain't so.")

Continuous learning requires embracing such explicit practices as the ones recommended in this book. Without such practices, what we call "knowledge" soon ossifies into a hardening of the cognitive arteries. The evidence is very suggestive that something like this is exactly what spawned Wall Street's Monster. How else to explain the utter absence of learning about the dangers of derivatives that followed the collapse of Long-Term Capital Management?

"Everything your immaterial mind imagines leaves material traces," writes Doidge. "Each thought alters the physical state of your brain synapses at a microscopic level. Each time you imagine moving your fingers across the keys to play the piano, you alter the tendrils in your living brain."

This has been stunningly documented in studies showing that mental and physical piano practice produce identical brain changes, and that imaginary physical exercise yields nearly as much gain in muscular strength as actual physical exercise—twenty-two percent versus thirty percent in one famous study cited by Dr. Doidge.

Quoting Alvaro Pascual-Leone, head of the Beth Israel Deaconess Medical Center at Harvard Medical School, Doidge points out the brain is "plastic, not elastic." By "plastic" Pascual-Leone means the brain is more like playdough than a rubber band; after you reshape it, it won't spring back to its former shape.

Once you form a habit or subscribe to a belief (like Greenspan's notion that self-regulation by financial companies is an effective way to protect the economy), your brain has created a neural pathway. The longer you've had the habit or belief, the deeper the path. It's easy to poke fun at Greenspan, who rejected contradictory evidence in order to remain faithful to his very own rut, but jealously guarding our beliefs is normal. *Unless*, that is, we adopt practices that prevent it.

Jealously guarding our beliefs is normal. Unless, that is, we adopt practices that prevent it.

Which illustrates the other side of the neuroplasticity coin. Neuroplasticity creates cognitive rigidity as easily as cognitive flexibility, Dr. Pascual-Leone notes.

"Is it possible, once 'tracks' or neural pathways have been laid down, to get out of those paths and onto different ones?" writes Dr. Doidge. "Yes, according to Pascual-Leone, but it is difficult because, once we have created these tracks, they become 'really speedy' and very efficient at guiding the [mental] sled down the hill. To take a different path becomes increasingly difficult. A roadblock of some kind is necessary to help us change direction."

The simple neural aids mentioned above represent just such roadblocks. The exercises contained in the following chapters offer others.

The happy news is that neural roadblocks can be small, incremental and quick. We don't need extensive training or workshops. Even "massive plastic reorganizations can occur at unexpected speed," writes Doidge. This is because, "a neuron's electrical signal often lasts a thousandth of a second." In that quicksilver twinkle of time, the living brain has continued to grow—in one direction or another.

Dr. Doidge recounts an unusual experiment at a Spanish boarding school, where teachers were blindfolded for a week in order to better understand their blind students. "A blindfold is a roadblock for the sense of sight, and within the week their tactile senses and their ability to judge space had become extremely sensitive. They were able to differentiate makes of motorcycles by the sounds of their engines and to distinguish objects in their paths by their echoes. When the teachers first removed their blindfolds, they were profoundly disoriented and couldn't judge space or see."

The practices included in this book amount to neural roadblocks to your habitual thinking. They allow the penetration of new data and creative problem-solving that otherwise would have been impossible.

At first glance, these practices are deceptively simple, and you may have an overwhelming instinct to read through but not *do* them. As Doidge points out, this is a normal response to the challenge of learning anything. Quoting Merzenich, he notes that learning requires attention, and attention takes incentive. You "must have enough of a reward, or punishment, to keep paying attention through what might otherwise be a boring training session," writes Doidge.

This is a critical understanding for leaders to have, as a December 15, 2008 special report *The Wall Street Journal* published in collaboration with the MIT Sloan Management Review made clear. In a story headlined "Lessons Learned: The key to effective training isn't necessarily what happens in the classroom. It's what you do afterward," the *Journal* reported, "Teaching employees new skills is one thing. Getting them to apply what they have learned is quite another.

"With some studies suggesting that just 10% to 40% of training is ever used on the job, it is clear that a big chunk of the tens of billions of dollars organizations spend annually on staff development is going down the drain.

"Chalk some of it up to human nature: Training involves change, and change creates anxiety that people seek to avoid. In other cases, old habits and workplace pressures can break down even the strongest resolve to use newly acquired skills and knowledge."

So where do you find the incentive needed to make training pay off, to follow practices like the ones recommended in this book? The best answer, Chapter Six argues, is deep within.

The process of escaping your neurological ruts and blazing new performance trails is analogous to latent physical capacity. You may have the ability to run a marathon if you train properly, but you still have to train. To train, you have to find the motivation. As the birth of Wall Street's Monster clearly suggests, anyone who would lead in today's environment who *cannot* find the motivation to change habitual patterns of thought and inspire others may

> Anyone who would lead in today's environment who cannot find the motivation to change habitual patterns of thought may as well come to work with an Old World seafarer's map of a flat Earth.

as well come to work with an Old World seafarer's map of a flat Earth.

On the other hand, neuroscience shows that those who can learn to approach our new environment by seizing the galactic power of brain plasticity to improve their performance are in for the most rewarding and exhilarating experience in human history, one in which the constant renewal of discovery offers the ultimate endorphin high.

INSTRUCTION MANUAL

The Angel in the Stone
*A chisel set for continuously
discovering, and displaying, your best self*

AS FINISHING TOUCHES were being applied to this book, U.S. Treasury Secretary Timothy Geithner explained to readers of *The Wall Street Journal* his plan for economic recovery. "The lack of an appropriate and modern regulatory regime and resolution authority helped cause this crisis," he wrote on March 23, 2009, saying that the crisis "will continue to constrain our capacity to address future crises until we put in place fundamental reforms."

I agree. But what are the most critically needed reforms? I believe they go well beyond mere monetary policy.

Three months after Geithner wrote his *Wall Street Journal* piece, President Barack Obama suggested that Wall Street's Monster had been unleashed by a "cascade of mistakes and missed opportunities which took place over the course of decades."

Yes, but what caused those mistakes and missed opportunities? I argue that the real cause was basically inadequate neural fitness on the part of those who made the mistakes and missed the opportunities. Obviously, these errors weren't passive—the mistakes didn't make themselves and the opportunities didn't miss themselves. The mistakes were made, and the opportunities were missed, the evidence suggests to me, because of a use of the mind that is no longer adequate to deal with the market, social, and political realities that the mind itself has wrought.

A hundred and ninety years ago, one Anton Diabelli, a prolific music composer and principal in the Viennese publishing company of Cappi and Diabelli, asked fifty or so of his contemporaries to compose a variation on a waltz he had written. His contemporaries had names like Schubert, Czerny, Hummel, Beethoven. Herr Diabelli planned to publish the resulting music to raise money for widows and orphans of the Napoleonic Wars.

Setting aside his work on the Missa Solemnis, Beethoven famously composed not one but thirty-three interpretations of Diabelli's waltz. Beethoven's Opus 120, now known as the Diabelli Variations, revolutionized the variation form.

We can only speculate about what sparked this mold-shattering creativity. I like to think it was simply an ode to the sheer cognitive joy of it. In any case, the discoveries of neuroscience suggest that the composition of a musical variation is something of a metaphor for every act in every moment of life.

How we are *inclined* to respond to any challenge is subject to our synaptic mold. That means our responses are set in plastic, not concrete. In every circumstance we are free to choose. The range of available variations is unlimited. We just need a strategy, a technique, for constantly tailoring our synaptic mold to meet our ever-changing challenges.

My concern about Geithner's optimistic words about building "a stronger system" is that they will likely prove empty unless leaders adopt a new thinking regimen. Otherwise, it's highly unlikely that people will escape the neural ruts that produced this crisis in the first place.

In other words, the way of thinking that produced the crisis in the first place will reliably replicate similar crises in the future. Causes cause causes that cause other causes. Any attempt to manage the causes and effects of today and tomorrow based only on yesterday's chain of events is doomed.

Former Procter & Gamble CEO A.G. Lafley reflected this point in the June 2009 *Harvard Business Review*. He quoted from Peter Drucker's book, *Management Challenges for the Twenty-First Century*: "One cannot *manage* change. One can only be ahead of it… In a period of upheavals, such as the one we are living in, change is the norm. To be sure, it is painful and risky, and above all it requires a great deal of very hard work. But unless it is seen as the task of the organization to *lead change*, the organization… will not survive."

The purpose of the following practices is to avoid the futility of trying to "manage" the future by providing a just-in-time regimen for synaptic molding. These practices are proven tools, "variation tools," you might call them, that can help you respond to any challenge in any moment with ever more alacrity. The practices address what I consider the most critical performance areas of leadership. Namely, authenticity, absolute personal accountability, courage, intent, and the ability to "create" truth with others, as circumstances demand.

The practices are not discrete. They overlap.

The practices are simple but not easy. Performing them blazes new synaptic trails in your own brain and in the brains of everyone touched by the ripples of your actions.

You do not perform these practices by just reading about them. Doing them takes physical action. To actually do them is to introduce an entirely new story to the world, a story the world desperately needs, a story uniquely your own.

These practices are designed to be used in the heat of the most important leadership moment: breakdowns. As I see it, breakdowns are boons, not beasts. They are nothing less than a built-in navigational aid, a subtle *beep-beep-beep* signaling the need for course correction. In the digital world we have created, the need for course correction is constant.

You will see in the practices that I urge you to journal and otherwise write things down. Most of us resist going to the trouble of doing this. That's because it takes two efforts, both doing it and creating the habit of doing it. Creating that new habit is where you create the new synapses, where you free yourself from the hardwiring of your subjectivity, where you create the new wiring of objectivity. Keeping a written journal makes you the author, not just the subject, of your story.

The new story that will emerge from your performance of these practices loosens in your mind the synaptic bonds of the past—those inevitable hereditary ties that make you a member of a privileged thinking tribe feeling its way through a mystery. To perform these practices is to replace miniscule byways with new ones that come from your own imagination and purpose, leading toward where you want to go.

For two reasons I can promise you that these practices work, elementary as they may seem. First, I constantly use them myself with life-sustaining results. In fact, I'd be lost without them. Second, I teach them to my clients and receive the continuous proof of their effectiveness. My colleague Mark Shunk, a former CEO client and veteran Honeywell executive, has a down-to-earth way of describing what happens. He said:

I first experienced these practices when Michael was my coach. The reason I'm such a believer and advocate is because of the transforming effect they had on me. It was like taking off a backpack filled with two hundred pounds of rock. These practices help me lead powerfully, being who I am. They help me attend to fundamental things all the time, and as a result being seen by those who I would seek to have follow me as being worthy of their trust. If you think of the world we live in, how many people would we see or deem as worthy of our trust? It's a short list. But all of us have the ability to be that person.

These practices remind me of that Michelangelo quote about seeing an angel in the stone and carving until he set the angel free. I've been to Florence and seen the incomplete Michelangelo sculpture that shows the figure of a man emerging from a big block of marble, chisel marks and all. It had a huge impact on me, because you could see the vision of the master bringing the man out of the stone.

We have within us tremendous power, which is often encased in the stone of what the world, or our experience, or our training, have told us we are *supposed* to be rather than who we are. And the tension is trying to lead out of a set of actions that may or may not be consistent with who I am.

And so this coaching work is about reaching into that and saying, "What is it that's binding you? Is it fear? Is it uncertainty about your own capability? Is it maintaining a pose? What is it that's preventing you from just standing on the firm foundation of who you are and the gifts you uniquely bring?"

Fear can be the thing that seizes us up and encases us in this immobilizing weight that keeps us from doing what we otherwise might do. It could be our own routine or habit of blaming others, rather than looking at our own accountability. Michael uses a phrase, "Everywhere you go, there you are." Even if I'm not a hundred percent responsible for what caused something to occur, am I ten percent responsible? And am I willing to be a hundred percent accountable for that ten percent? If I continue to not get from others around me what I want, well, could the consistent element be my own leadership?

The practices in this book are chisels that can chip away at the figurative stone that confines us. In helping my clients use these practices, I want to help them become the leader that I think God created them to be. That leader is embodied in the skills and capabilities and aptitudes that the stone of our habits keeps locked inside us. These practices help us see ourselves truly in a different way than we have seen ourselves before, not In our flawlessness, or our effort to appear to be flawless, but in our flawedness. They let us recognize that we aren't perfect and don't need to be perfect to be powerful as a leader. They let us acknowledge our shortcomings, accentuate our strengths, and lead from there.

When I think of the leaders who have been most powerful in my own life, it wasn't so much that I was so astonished by their skill set. It was that I believed in who they were. I trusted them and was willing to put myself on the same path. That made me committed to doing my very best for them, and it allowed me to generate more than I thought was possible.

I walk into the offices of leaders with dozens of leadership books on their shelves, and yet they are frustrated because their leadership isn't working. These *Quicksilver* practices help them see, and become, who they might be that others would choose to follow.

I can vouch for our clients' assessment of Mark, because of what they tell me. It's Mark's unflagging authenticity that has sometimes led clients to dispatch their corporate aircraft to ensure his presence at critical meetings.

Mark epitomizes the truth about the practices that follow. What gives them their ability to change your life, and the lives of those you touch, is your willingness to attempt them without reservation. You will not perfect them. That isn't possible. But the difference between not attempting them at all and attempting them earnestly is so great as to approach, if not a form of perfection, at least the nobility that great leadership requires. This attempt, I believe, is a prelude to miracles.

Because I earn my living teaching leaders to control their thoughts, it's fair for you to wonder whether I control mine. It's fair to wonder that, too, about the person I asked to help me write this book.

In both our cases, life has given us experiences in which controlling our thoughts was (and remains) the best option.

My thought-clarifying experience began in early 1997

with a tingling sensation in my arms and hands. To give a long story the brevity I allot it, it turned out that I had multiple sclerosis, a degenerative disease of the central nervous system.

I was a superbly fit, athletic forty-two-year-old, in love with life, my family, my business. My biggest problem wasn't the unwelcome news of the disease (life happens), but that it didn't fit into any category of possibility or meaning acceptable to me.

So I created meaning. I would have MS. It would not have me.

I have it by adhering to the innovative treatment regimen created by my conventional and holistic neurologists and by thinking the kind of generative thoughts advocated in this book. When I feel the telltale tingling of symptoms, I take it as a signal to create—to go for a jog, meditate, envision my wife and myself sitting on a beach playing with our future grandchildren, living precisely the life I intend to live. So far, so good.

Larry's experience was a little different. It came in the middle of an intense Tet Offensive rocket and mortar attack during the Vietnam War.

"This is hard," said a voice in his head. "If you get through this, nothing will ever be hard again."

The promise of that thought settled him. It wasn't as though he chose the thought. The thought somehow chose him. It was a stroke of luck he instantly seized on. It let him concentrate on his job from a different perspective. With that flash of insight he recognized that he was not the events he was experiencing, even though they could take him away in a heartbeat. He was the "experiencer," the events' keeper. The difference remains a benefaction that has never left him. It lets him keep the indelible memories of war instead of being kept by them. With such a tactic is PTSD managed. Events have no power to stress us after the fact, much less cause disorder, without our permission. The power to assign their effect on us is ours alone.

CHAPTER THREE

BE ABSOLUTELY ACCOUNTABLE

True freedom comes with understanding that we alone are the authors of every event, scene, chapter, and outcome in our lives.

"Liberty means responsibility.
That is why most men dread it."
—GEORGE BERNARD SHAW

LEADERSHIP, AS I DEFINE IT, is a relationship that rests on the absolute accountability of the leader. It means that a leader's accountability is not contingent upon the actions of others.

This approach to leadership involves constantly monitoring the performance of others, noting when and where performance needs adjustment in response to changing conditions. It requires maintaining a list of actions one can take to support the changes being requested of colleagues—and then, of course, constantly taking those actions.

This is an extremely dynamic process. It takes the highest level of engagement on the part of the leader. It takes a selfless willingness to change oneself to help others change themselves in order to continually rise to the demands of the ever-changing marketplace.

The purpose of absolute accountability, in other words, is

to help people do the hardest thing they ever do: change. Think about it. Change means doing something new. A leader who is helping colleagues do something new is, of necessity, also doing something new. This is change by collaboration, not fiat.

Such an embrace of accountability can come from only one place: the leader's choice. It is purely personal and completely voluntary; no one can impose it on you.

Leaders who, in the silence of their minds, betroth themselves to absolute accountability must repeat their vows not just daily, but repeatedly throughout the day.

This is the most powerful, creative, life-giving, hopeful way of being in the world I know of.

It is a journey, not a destination.

Absolute personal accountability creates relationships that fundamentally differ from most relationships. Most relationships turn on conditional accountability.

It is a process by which leaders constantly monitor the needs of the organization, and then, beginning with themselves, attend to the endless suite of changes needed to meet those needs. It is a shepherd's life.

This is a fundamentally different approach to leadership than merely tapping one's education and experience and invoking the hierarchical authority of one's position. It requires the most intimate kind of continuing education.

Absolute personal accountability creates relationships that fundamentally differ from most relationships. Most relationships turn on conditional accountability: "I, Joe, will do my job so long as Tom does his." Or, "I, Josephine, will be able to report a quarterly profit to the board, as long as Sales delivers on projections." Or, "I, Frank, will fix the porch as soon as you, Mary, clean the basement."

In friendships, marriages, the workplace, that is a formula for breakdown. It guarantees one unpleasantness after another along a spectrum ranging from nuisance to failure.

Why? For one thing, in such a relationship, your responsibility is purely subjective: The Other defines it. And if The Other says the relationship is not producing the desired results because you aren't doing what you ought to, the relationship breaks down. The consequence of the breakdown depends on what's at stake.

Beyond that, leadership ends the moment the leader breaks off a relationship.

Absolute accountability keeps leaders in the hunt for answers, and that's what they get paid for. Leaders stop leading when they make others fully responsible for breakdowns.

Accountability is the very source of leadership power. Rank may be the source of authority, but there is no creative power in authority alone. Power is a function of accountability, which in this context is the promise to produce results—*no matter what.*

> Power is a function of accountability, which in this context is the promise to produce results—no matter what.

When leaders declare breakdowns because subordinates don't do as they should, you have dramaturgy, not leadership. This isn't always the case, but it happens enough to unleash monsters of every description.

When things go wrong, what typically happens is that

we automatically (defensively) blame others. The fixing of blame may be accurate, but, by itself, it is not leadership. It is impotence.

The fixing of blame may be accurate, but, by itself, it is not leadership. It is impotence.

The operative word is Should. Joe Leader *could* use another word. And he/she *could* use it differently.

Josephine Leader might say: "What could I do that would assist Tom?"

The importance of this simple substitution cannot be overemphasized.

With apologies to the old English nursery rhyme:

FOR WANT OF A COULD THE COMPANY WAS LOST

For want of a Could the solution was lost.
For want of a solution the opportunity was lost.
For want of opportunity market share was lost.
For want of market share profit was lost.
For want of profit the company was lost.
All for the want of a Could.

One need look no further than General Motors for an example of a company being lost for want of a Could. The December 1, 2008, *Fortune* magazine cover story, "GM: Death of an American Dream," illustrated that tragedy poignantly.

"Ask [GM CEO] Rick Wagoner why GM isn't more like Toyota, and he'd tell you, 'We're playing our own game—taking advantage of our own unique heritage and strengths.' Turns out GM should have forgotten that and become more like Toyota. Toyota's market cap is now $103.6 billion; GM's is $1.8 billion."

Obviously, GM *could* have tried to benchmark Toyota. In failing to lead GM in such an endeavor, Wagoner clearly succumbed to his synaptic mold. Sticking to "our own game" shrunk his company's working capital to two percent of its most powerful rival.

If there is one way to "not be conformed to this world, but be transformed by the renewal of your mind" *(Romans 12:2),* changing Shoulds to Coulds is it. And if there is one technique that stands above all others in the bag of tricks my colleagues and I use to coach executives, this also is it.

> If there is one way to "not be conformed to this world, but be transformed by the renewal of your mind," changing Shoulds to Coulds is it.

Changing Shoulds to Coulds is the ultimate just-in-time, or continuous time, tool of conscious leadership.

To declare that something *should not be* a certain way is life's ultimate whine. It is a variation on the ancient lament, "The world isn't fair; it shouldn't be this way."

There shouldn't be hurricanes, viruses, mosquitoes, innovative competitors…

Such thinking, in any setting, guarantees personal impotence, despair, suffering of every imaginable type. Again, the suffering leads all the way from momentary irritation to loss of precious relationships to, in the most extreme cases, suicide or fatal, stress-caused diseases.

Psychologist Albert Ellis considered the imperatives "should," "must," and "ought" to be tyrants of our own creation.

In a chorus of victimhood, people "should" all over themselves all the time, said Ellis. They drive themselves crazy.

A founder of cognitive therapy, Ellis is considered a psychology giant equal in stature to Freud. In the mid-1950s, Ellis developed what today is called "rational emotive behavior therapy" as a way of helping his patients see that their own thoughts about their circumstances—not the circumstances themselves—fire their emotions and drive their behavior.

What leaders do in the three seconds, three minutes, three hours after they notice breakdowns—right there, that instant: that's the leadership moment!

"I started pointing out their irrational demands and disputing their shoulds and musts," Ellis said of his patients, "and some of them got remarkably better quite quickly."

In fact, so many of Dr. Ellis's patients were so quickly freed from their personal demons that the cognitive therapy he pioneered is now a cornerstone of psychotherapy. "The prince of reason," *Psychology Today* called Ellis a few years ago.

The truth is, the executives I've worked with over the past quarter century have all had the basic skills required by their posts. And that includes knowing when to outsource. Because, you know what? If you're not good at strategy, just hire McKinsey & Company. They'll give you a strategy.

But you can't hire McKinsey to talk you and your subordinates through your breakdowns. There's nobody there but you. You can't subcontract this aspect of leadership. You can give an inspirational speech every quarter, but what do you do the next day when your top lieutenants aren't inspired anymore?

What leaders do in the three seconds, three minutes, three hours after they notice breakdowns large and small that foreshadow results they don't want—right there, that instant: that's the leadership moment! What a leader does in that moment marks the difference between an effective leader and a failed leader.

If you choose to hold yourself absolutely accountable for the performance of your colleagues, your thoughts and actions will be different than the older, hierarchical model. You will ask yourself, "What do I want them to do, and how can I support them?" And then you will make your requests and offer your support. And you will ask them what other support they need, and you might negotiate over providing it.

> Choosing to be a conscious, absolutely accountable leader means choosing to free yourself from your limiting story.

The instant you tell yourself that another *should* do something differently than what they've already done, you have taken two serious missteps.

First, you have entered into a fiction. Because that "should" exists in only one place in the known universe: inside your own story of the situation. Your own story is merely an artifact of your humanity, a thought product of your particular synaptic legacy. However logical your story may be, it is too restricted to let you respond to the real-life dynamic and unpredictable environment as creatively as possible. In other words, choosing to be a conscious, absolutely accountable leader means choosing to free yourself from your limiting story. And it means choosing to help your colleagues throw off their own synaptic shackles by first throwing off yours in front of them.

Second, you have stopped leading. There are absolutely times when the decision to stop leading someone is the right decision. But, because of its terminal nature, it is the most extreme decision a leader ever makes. Before you choose to stop leading (either by blaming others, ignoring a breakdown, or firing someone), there are usually a number of more hopeful options to be explored.

To ask yourself what you could do to support others in performing as you need them to perform—and to ask it again and again and again—unleashes creativity. Your mind is your most loyal subordinate, a veritable genie. If you ask it a question and mean it—if you inquire with true burning curiosity—your mind will work tirelessly, 24/7, to bring you an answer.

In other words, your mind will endlessly transform you with its own constant renewal. One way to think of this is as a kind of ongoing recalibration that invites others to join you. But here's the catch: your mind will recalibrate only at your request. Your mind is far too dependable an autopilot to divert itself without input from you.

Your mind will recalibrate only at your request. Your mind is far too dependable an autopilot to divert itself without input from you.

So if you habitually declare breakdowns to be caused by others who aren't doing, according to your personal narrative, what they *should* do, then there is no question for your mind to answer, no problem for it to solve.

That's why you stop leading the moment you simply blame someone.

Conversely, recognition that another *could* do something differently, and perhaps you could do something to help him, is the road less traveled, the one that, as Robert Frost said, makes all the difference.

Inspired leadership is a kind of alchemy, in my opinion. And Coulds are the philosopher's stone that transform the lead of human imperfection into the gold of human possibility.

Choosing to hold yourself absolutely accountable for the performance of others does not relieve *them* of accountability and responsibility for their own actions.

One of the most important differences between the Could Road and the Should Road is that the former leads to a future of one's choice; the latter is either stuck in the dead past or in an illusion of the future. Who can say with certainty what "should" be done? Why should it be done? Based on what assumptions? Such conditions are inevitably speculative and uncertain. To say something "could" be done, however, is more inherently accurate, concrete and creative.

> The energy of "Could" is positive and expansive; it is the thrust of possibility. The energy of "Should" is negative and restrictive; it is the barrier of obligatory confinement.

When you focus on what someone should have done in the past, or should do in the future, you are addressing either a time to which there is never any return, or a future to which there is never any real access.

The energy of "Could" is positive and *expansive;* it is the thrust of possibility. The energy of "Should" is negative and restrictive; it is the barrier of obligatory confinement. To the extent you Should on yourself and others, you dwell in the foul air of regret. You subject yourself to the hounds of frustration and depression, running a gauntlet of nasty risks both mental and physical. Frustration is not creative. Depression makes you sick.

The Could Road, by contrast, to borrow a phrase from Winston Churchill, traverses the sunlit uplands of the eternal now. It is always about the infinite possibility of improvement. For Josephine Leader to ask what could be done to support Tom's improvement is empowering to all concerned.

Because, as her coach, I work for Josephine, I do not concern myself with Tom. Were I assigned to work with Tom, I would try to help him understand where he breaks himself off from keeping his agreements, where he takes the Should exit instead of staying on the golden Could thruway.

But Tom is not my concern. By helping Josephine understand that Should is a leadership death spiral, and that Could is the way to never-ending possibilities, I constantly live in the hope that Josephine can lead Tom to the same insight.

And that makes me deeply happy. What a critical mass of such transformative renewal would mean to a group of any size—family, organization, society—is truly inspiring to contemplate.

Like the other practices in this book, the one for developing absolute accountability may seem simplistic. But that is a deceptive impression. Understanding how to be absolutely accountable is easy. Becoming absolutely accountable isn't. It requires determination and persistence, because it involves replacing one very powerful habit with another. It also involves harnessing the ego.

When Alan Greenspan was peppered with questions by Congress in a four-hour interrogation on October 23, 2008, he was unable to accept responsibility for his part in the financial collapse. He blamed bankers. He could barely admit he had even made a mistake. He did not apologize, even though the nation was horrified at what had befallen the economy under his watch.

With this amount of blood in the water, media sharks and comedians could be expected to hit immediately. They did. Greenspan predictably became the butt of jokes. Some of them (like the shtick performed by Jon Stewart on the October 24, 2008, broadcast of the *Daily Show*) were surprisingly off-color even for the most irreverent company.

Stewart wound up his gag on a note suitable for family viewing, however. He showed a clip of Greenspan's Congressional testimony in which he reiterated that his trust in bankers to police themselves had been misplaced. In a masterful stroke of irony that gains resonance with reflection, Stewart opined that it would have been better had bankers chained money to the little kiosks in bank foyers instead of the courtesy ink pens they provide for customers. Bankers didn't trust their customers not to steal their pens. But Congress, Greenspan and the Clinton Administration trusted bankers not to steal the wealth of nations.

The instruction-manual section of this book is intended to help you avoid the failure and humiliation that besmirches Greenspan's legacy. Before moving on to the accountability practice, though, I want to add two important caveats.

The point is, to choose not to lead is very different from the default of not choosing, because you're unconsciously caught up in the internal melodrama of your habitual thought processes.

The first concerns the decision to stop leading someone. The simple truth is, you can become a virtuoso at illuminating Coulds, and sometimes you will just run out of them. Every now and then I will help a client assemble an exhaustive set of Coulds that leads to the realization that they've all been tried in one way or another. At those times, the appropriate choice is to stop offering leadership. Meaning that the correct action is to either fire the subordinate or, if firing is not possible for whatever reason, to move the individual out of the role in which he/she is not performing.

Absolute accountability, in other words, is not a panacea. Nor does it reflect a Pollyannish view of life. It doesn't always yield the desired outcome. What it does always yield, however, is continuously improving leadership skills. It keeps practitioners optimistic and creative.

The point is, to choose not to lead is very different from the default of not choosing, when you're unconsciously caught up in the internal melodrama of your habitual thought processes. To do the latter is to be held fast in your synaptic mold. That is a form of being lived by the story you inherited, instead of choosing to create the story that best serves you and your company now.

The second caveat is a variation on "physician, heal thyself." Absolute accountability, replacing Shoulds with Coulds, is a powerful change tool, a means of continuous recalibration. But make no mistake: absolute accountability is about change. And change is stressful. When you want to get people to change, you will encounter resistance.

If you want your people to think or behave in any way that's significantly different from what they're already doing, they're going to resist. You will feel it. How you deal with their resistance will determine how readily people will follow you—or even if they will follow you at all.

Among other things, absolute accountability can take you into what Daniel Goleman calls "zones of tacitly denied information." If you think they don't exist in your organization, you're probably kidding yourself. There is hardly a richer vein for any leader to explore, because it's where potential disaster tends to hide. But to lead people into these shadowy caves requires a leader who will set an example. If anybody is going to be good at this recalibration—a recalibration that is no more and no less than constant, honest self-inquiry—it had better be the leader.

PRACTICE

Change Shoulds to Coulds

MAKE A LIST OF THE TOP several breakdowns you are now dealing with. (Typically, people have anywhere from two to five breakdowns that they can put their fingers on immediately.)

These will involve upsets, complaints, brooding concerns about unmet expectations, broken agreements, disruptive conflicts among colleagues, etc. Some are banal. Some are ominous.

As an example of the banal, assume an unfamiliar noise is coming from your car's suspension. This *shouldn't* be happening; the car just came from the repair shop, and the mechanic found nothing wrong.

Or, let's say you're an investment bank CEO and one of your directors, Frank, took a week off to play in a bridge tournament instead of attending special meetings on your company's exposure to sub-prime mortgage-based securities.

Obviously, both breakdowns could run the gamut from trivial to catastrophic.

Now, choose one breakdown to work on. In the case of the mechanic, begin by listing his actions. Thus, he changed the oil and performed a complete vehicle inspection. Write out all the Shoulds associated with the breakdown: the mechanic should have thoroughly checked the car, the engine, the transmission, brakes, tires, chassis, etc. He *should* have found the suspension problem before giving you back the car.

These Shoulds will be about others, yourself, or even life in general. Write them all down. (Remember, writing is more effective synaptic rewiring than just thinking about them.) You now have your story of the breakdown.

Note that the bigger you perceive the breakdown to be, the greater the number of Shoulds you will have.

Now, scratch out the Shoulds and replace them with Coulds. Thus:

"The mechanic *could* check the car more thoroughly."

"Frank *could* attend emergency meetings on our pending sub-prime mortgage crisis."

Next, for every Should/Could conversion make a note of actions you might consider to help the other party to take appropriate action. You want to identify what you *could* do such that others would be more likely to take the actions you want. These notes might include requests to make of the other party or offers of support. Thus:

"I could take out a notebook and write down the precise circumstances when I hear the suspension noise in order to give the mechanic more to go on. Then I could offer the mechanic my list and ask him to replicate the conditions (making a sharp left turn, etc.) in which I detect the noise."

Or:

"I could request a meeting with Frank and review with him our conclusions about financial risks and my concern about our sub-prime exposure. I could ask him to study our findings, then do his own research and offer recommendations."

In nurturing optimum teamwork, leaders are often called upon to mediate disputes and breakdowns among key colleagues. Instead of issuing the edict that a particular breakdown shouldn't be happening, a leader could ask what he or she could do to help mend it. This can include actions like putting on the table the leader's knowledge of the situation and requesting direct conversations about it until all the facts are known and the conflicting perspectives are reconciled. I've never known a case in which the lists of Coulds in such circumstances are not extensive enough to facilitate resolution in one way or another. And the resolution, even if it's as regrettable as having to fire someone, is always prefer-able to having a conflict fester and become infectious simply because it "shouldn't" exist.

Before going further, please notice two things.

First, reflect on the different moods associated with the Shoulds and Coulds. Chances are, the Shoulds brought the negative emotion caused by the frustration of not getting what you want. The Coulds were probably associated with the positive emotion of hope.

Second, notice how you feel about doing the practice. If you did it in a spirit of openness and curiosity, you may have experienced a pleasant buzz, however slight. That's a little endorphin squirt, a tiny shot of natural morphine to reward you for your effort. All learning produces a high.

Also, the simple step of doing the practice created a new synaptic connection in your brain. That may have felt good, too. It's not exactly the birth of a star in the galaxy of human affairs, but it is a mote of new stardust.

The next step is to apply your new understanding to the actual breakdowns on your list. As with any new skill, start small and build from your experience.

Chapter Four

BE (REALLY) BRAVE

The World's Terrible Lie About Courage

"This man [John Wayne] was a symbol of the fake machismo we had come to hate…"
—William Manchester

MOST OF MY CLIENTS ARE NOT BRAVE. I don't mean they're cowards. I mean they don't have a healthy and effective relationship with fear. Most people don't. This is a serious problem, because no character trait is more valuable than real courage. Especially for leaders.

Similarly, no disability is more crippling than unmanaged fear. Note the qualifier. You can't prevent fear, and you wouldn't want to. Fear keeps you alive and healthy. You can only manage fear, but you can't do that until you de-stigmatize it.

> No disability is more crippling than unmanaged fear.

Paradoxically, mismanaging fear can make you sick or even kill you. That's right, fear sometimes kills.

Managing fear—first noticing it, then choosing your response to it—is true courage.

> Managing fear—first noticing it, then choosing your response to it—is true courage.

Fear is a reflex. It flashes throughout the body in milliseconds. A perceived threat activates the brain's amygdala, which recruits the hypothalamus to flush the hormone corticotropin-releasing factor, which shoots a message to the pituitary and adrenal glands to inject the stress hormones epinephrine (adrenaline), norepinephrine and cortisol into the bloodstream. These powerful chemicals arm the body to fight or flee.

> You want to have your fear so it doesn't have you. That's your only choice. And forget about not choosing, because that's also a choice.

Simultaneously, the amygdala archives the experience in the body's synaptic files for future reference. Fear molds you, in other words, and predisposes you to future behavior. If you've ever been shot at, yelled at and hit, barked at and bitten by a dog, choked by saltwater while being tumbled by a big wave, or had any other similarly "memorable" experience, you understand: you can't prevent fear, but you can prevent it from taking control of your life.

That's the key: you want to have your fear so it doesn't have you. That's your only choice. And forget about not choosing, because that's also a choice. Fear has you triangulated.

There's something else about fear that is especially important for leaders to understand. Not only is it reflexive, it's also contagious.

"When danger lurks, fear spreads through a crowd as body postures alter in rapid cascade from one individual to the next." That was the language of a 2004 National Academy of Sciences paper entitled "Fear fosters flight: A mechanism for fear contagion when perceiving emotion expressed by a whole body."

Think of flocks of birds, schools of fish, herds of ungulates bolting as a single organism in response to perceived threat.

As if body language weren't enough, your fear pheromones will also communicate with everyone within olfactory range of you. That's why there can sometimes be so much fear in a room that you can smell it.

This is where our emerging knowledge of the brain approaches the mystical. When we consider that each of the neocortex's hundred billion neurons has as many as twenty thousand connections to other brain cells, and that those cells connect with millions of other body cells, and that, as neuroscientists helpfully point out, the potential permutations of these connections exceed the number of molecules in the known universe, we are only beginning to grasp the reality of our circumstances.

Those sitting with the *drip-drip-drip* of unmanaged fear actually may be carriers of a kind of airborne virus.

Next, we have to factor in the connection between the galactic power grid of our own brains with the power grids of everyone else's. Talk about a wireless network!

Now think of the implications of this physiological reality for the success of any organization. Those sitting with the *drip-drip-drip* of unmanaged fear actually may be carriers of a kind of airborne virus.

Bottom line: unmanaged fear not only destroys self-confidence and creativity, and sucks the joy out of life, along the way it destroys the body. That is because adrenaline, that fight or flight rocket fuel, is metabolized—burned up—in the presence of oxygen. A loud noise triggers the release of adrenaline, but so do poor third-quarter results, climbing gas prices, the threat of terrorism, "toxic" debt obligations, defective O-rings. The list is endless. The problem with the latter kind of stress is that you incur it while sitting down. Because you're not fleeing or fighting, you're not taking in additional oxygen to help you burn up the adrenaline. Nevertheless, you must clear the adrenaline from your system, because it has you on red alert, disrupting your vital functions.

The stress hormone cortisol handles the adrenaline cleanup in these circumstances, neutralizing it chemically. The problem with cortisol's chemical mop-up of adrenaline is its nasty side effect. Cortisol breaks down muscle tissue, which is why chronic stress is linked to heart attacks.

"Israel recorded nearly 100 excess deaths during Saddam's 1991 Scud missile attacks—not from bomb injuries but from heart attacks presumably triggered by fear and stress," reported *Time* magazine February 23, 2003. "And a recent study suggests that heart patients around New York City suffered life-threatening heart arrhythmias at more than twice the usual rate in the month following the World Trade Center attack." Many didn't think of themselves as especially fearful.

Evidence like this also shows why there is both a grain of literal truth and dangerous misconception in many of the familiar admonitions about fear that shape our understanding of courage. As anyone who has ever witnessed it can attest, courage is a very real force in human affairs. It balances reflexive self-interest and deeply rooted individual survival instincts in a way that serves group survival.

But we have a bad habit of caricaturing courage in our movies. We mythologize courage in literature. We obfuscate it in oratory.

"The only thing we have to fear is fear itself," declared FDR in his first inaugural address.

"I must not fear," begins the Bene Gesserit litany in the science fiction classic *Dune*. "Fear is the mind killer. Fear is the little death that brings total obliteration…."

Fear, writes Yann Martel in *The Life of Pi*, "is life's only true opponent. Only fear can defeat life. It is a clever, treacherous adversary…."

While these exhortations are taken out of context, and while the full context of each contains profound wisdom, the ringing condemnations of fear as a mortal enemy are what tend to take root in the psyche and culture, shaming every sniveling, yellow-bellied cur of a chicken-hearted no-account who feels fear.

Too late! Too late! Too late! the brain responds to each of these stirring calls to be not afraid. You're already afraid! Now what are you going to do, deny it, and make yourself a liar, too?

Roosevelt went on to explain that he was talking about "nameless, unreasoning, unjustified terror which paralyzes needed efforts to convert retreat into advance."

From our earliest days, and in so many ways, we're taught to stuff away our fears. If we can't, the great liars tell us, we're failures.

The Bene Gesserit litany continues: "I will face my fear. I will permit it to pass over me and through me. And when it has gone past I will turn the inner eye to see its path. Where the fear has gone there will be nothing. Only I will remain."

And in *The Life of Pi*, Martel continues that fear, "real fear, such as shakes you to your foundation, such as you feel when you are brought face to face with your mortal end, nestles in your memory like a gangrene: it seeks to rot everything, even the words with which to speak of it. So you must fight hard to express it. You must fight hard to shine the light of words upon it. Because if you don't, if your fear becomes a wordless darkness that you avoid, perhaps even manage to forget, you open yourself to further attacks of fear because you never truly fought the opponent who defeated you."

There is a clear contradiction in each of these famous passages. They command the listener to both not fear and manage fear. Obviously, if you could banish fear, you wouldn't have to manage it.

But you can't banish it. And on this subject the world often tells us a terrible lie. From our earliest days, and in so many ways, we're taught to stuff away our fears. If we can't, the great liars tell us, we're failures.

Soldiers who have their noses rubbed in the truth about fear tend to be more contemptuous of this deceit than anyone. Take William Manchester, the famous historian. Manchester wrote that he once "had the enormous pleasure" of seeing the actor John Wayne "humiliated in person."

It happened at a Hawaiian Naval hospital where the worst casualties of the Pacific during World War II were sent. Manchester, a sergeant with the 29th Marines (a regiment that lost eighty percent of its Okinawa landing force) was one of those casualties. "Between Iwo Jima and Okinawa, the Marine Corps was being bled white," Manchester wrote in his 1987 essay, "Okinawa: The Bloodiest Battle of All."

For the rest of his life, encysted near his heart, Manchester carried a bullet and enough shrapnel to set off airport metal detectors. And embedded with the metal was a piece of the shinbone of a Marine—"The best man in my section"—who was "blown to pieces" while standing next to Manchester, "and the slime of his viscera enveloped me."

Manchester continued, "Each evening, Navy corpsmen would carry litters down to the hospital theater so the men could watch a movie. One night they had a surprise for us. Before the film the curtains parted and out stepped John Wayne, wearing a cowboy outfit—ten-gallon hat, bandanna, checkered shirt, two pistols, chaps, boots and spurs. He grinned his aw-shucks grin, passed a hand over his face and said, 'Hi ya, guys!' He was greeted by a stony silence. Then somebody booed. Suddenly everyone was booing.

"This man was a symbol of the fake machismo we had come to hate… And so we weren't macho. Yet we never doubted the justice of our cause…."

Manchester was discharged from the Marines with one hundred percent disability. As his retelling of that experience makes clear, it put him on intimate terms with fear. As the medal he received for "gallantry in action and extraordinary achievement" from his division commander attests, he was no stranger to real bravery, either. "Your courage was a constant source of inspiration," read the citation.

If anyone was qualified to talk about the difference between true courage and its Hollywood version, it was Manchester.

So, if true courage is not the absence of fear but its mastery, is there any proof we can see with our own eyes? As it happens, there is. It was entered into the cultural record on September 11, 2001.

In the summer of that year, Gedeon and Jules Naudet, French brothers who came to America to study film, were making a documentary about a New York City fire cadet. Their footage captured the actions of some of the first firemen on the scene after the terrorist attacks on the World Trade Center. Jules shot the only known footage of the first plane hitting Tower One.

The brothers, along with the firemen they were filming, narrowly escaped the fate of the three hundred forty-three other New York City firemen killed in the attack. In the course of making "9/11," a film considered by many to be history's greatest documentary, the Naudets preserved a rare visual archive of what managed fear— real courage—actually looks like in the presence of great physical danger.

> Fear-based self-absorption is not a character flaw. It is not "egotism."

The expression on the firemen's faces says it all. They were afraid. And still they did their jobs.

"Hope is the thing with feathers that perches in the soul" wrote Emily Dickinson. If so, unmanaged fear is the chimera, "a wordless darkness" squatting nearby, that keeps hope grounded or "paralyzed," as FDR put it.

Not only is chronic fear as destructive to the health of leaders as to everyone else, and not only is it contagious, but fear triggers self-absorption. And chronic self-absorption is fatal to leadership. But let me be very clear about this: fear-based self-absorption is not a character flaw. It is not "egotism."

On the contrary, it is an organic expression of the design brilliance of Mother Nature. Fear's purpose is to prevent your removal from the gene pool. Mother Nature is the ultimate Jewish mother. She gave you fear because she likes your genes. She wouldn't have created them otherwise. And she doesn't want you to go squandering them foolishly.

Fear is supposed to make you self-absorbed. It is supposed to get your attention in order to prompt the kind of action that will keep you around to tell your grandkids stories about that time you got really scared (or needlessly worried) and what you did about it, and how, well, maybe there's a moral in that tale for them.

So if right about now you are remembering some occasion on which you were quietly scared, and the fear made you self-absorbed, and your self-absorption caused you to behave in a way that even now burns your cheeks with embarrassment and curdles your spirit with guilt, I have two things to say to you.

One: Welcome to the human race.

Two: Stop it! Stop it right now!

I'm trying to make a point that will help you become really brave. Were your company paying me to sit with you at this moment as your executive coach, I would remind you that you're not getting paid the big bucks to guilt trip yourself. And I'm getting paid to help you earn the big bucks.

There is one consideration above all others that, in my opinion, makes true courage not just a leadership virtue but also a leadership necessity. (And true courage—I'm going to make myself tedious with repetition—is a healthy relationship with fear.) And here it is: effective leadership often scares people. This is because it asks them to change. And the prospect of change, given the brain's structure, is scary. If the threat of change is big enough, it sets off fight-or-flight warning bells. But even rumors of minor change, deep in the mysterious synaptic labyrinth of the psyche, stir a nervous chorus of whispers: *Careful! Watch it!*

I believe it comes down to this: any person who does not maintain a vigorous personal program of fear mastery is probably not qualified to lead. I know that sounds harsh, but I think it's true.

Any person who does not maintain a vigorous personal program of fear mastery is probably not qualified to lead.

And here's the kicker. The kind of fear I'm talking about isn't the kind caused by burning buildings and bloody battles. It's everyday, mundane, garden-variety anxiety that inevitably results from simply living, and in the process listening to the whispering chorus of worries.

Shakespeare did not write rousing band-of-brothers speeches to celebrate the courage needed to manage this form of fear. Bards don't sing of it; Tom Cruise doesn't get paid millions to act it out; novelists don't immortalize it; shrines aren't erected in its memory.

And yet, day in and day out, this is the overwhelming type of fear that confronts us. After all, when was the last time you had to rush into a flaming building? Or charge a hill under enemy fire?

On the other hand, when was the last time you felt your spirits sink without exactly knowing why? Or suffered silently under a private cloud of doubt, or kept quiet so as to avoid speaking an unwelcome truth or voicing an inconvenient concern? If you noticed something like a feeling of dread creep over you, did you even know where it came from? And then what happened? Did you let it prey on your mind? Or—powerful positive thinker that you are—did you simply put it out of your mind with your favorite distraction?

If you've worked on this issue before, you might know how to open the escape hatch, the powerful alternative to unconsciousness. Perhaps you were able to bring the worry into focus, identify its cause, and then consciously choose a constructive option to manage it. That is, quietly take charge of the emotion.

If you can do this, congratulations. In my opinion, that is true heroism. You practiced true courage. Do that enough and you will transform your life. And you will set an example for others to follow. And a critical mass of people inside your company acting that way—and critical masses are tiny—would make the company electrically creative in the presence of challenge.

If you doubt that, ask yourself how Wall Street's Monster, or any other business or economic challenge, would be affected by a critical mass of true courage.

> One of the biggest challenges we often face in managing fear is simply recognizing it for what it is in the first place.

"All organizational change is based on individual transformation," Peter Drucker once said. Clearly, there is no transformation so profound as becoming truly brave. It takes discipline. It's not natural—not for individuals, not for groups. It requires making a decision to master the powerful fight-or-flight reflex.

But how do you know when to defuse your fear? It's an important question, because one of the biggest challenges we often face in managing fear is simply recognizing it for what it is in the first place. While fear operates under many guises, it comes in only two forms: fight or flight.

When fear expresses itself physiologically, you know it. The adrenaline pumps, your heart races, your nerves stand on end, you break out in a sweat. When that happens, there's no doubt that you face a decision about what to do. Undoubtedly the more camouflaged variety of fear is trickier. Either way, you'll have fight-or-flight responses.

In the executive suite, the fight side of fear is commonly seen as anger and its many variations. Typical combative reactions toward others are irritability, impatience, sarcasm, demands, criticism, condescension—all are rooted in fear.

The flight impulse is subtler. Symptoms are emotional withdrawal from colleagues, which can take many forms. These include disinterest in the views of others and rehearsing conversations with others instead of trusting your spontaneity. Similarly, rationalizing, minimizing and denying concerns about colleagues' conduct is a sign of flight, as are stifling expression and repressing feelings about it. Reluctance to accept criticism from colleagues is also a form of flight.

Persistent bad moods signal chronic fear. Are you often annoyed, irritable, resentful, disappointed, resigned, distrustful, pessimistic, sad, depressed? If so, be alert; such feelings are kerosene at the roots of effective leadership. They lead to more of the same rather than to creativity. A mood is a state of enhanced neurological readiness to re-experience the same emotion again. You become annoyance-waiting-to-happen. Repetition improves the mind's performance—it's called learning—even of destructive things.

Behaviorally, both the fight and flight sides of fear tend to exhibit an ugly cultural gender bias. "Real men" don't get scared. A frightened man is a wimp. Men are allowed to get angry, though; he-men are even permitted to shout and curse in their meetings. "Good women," on the other hand, don't get angry. An angry woman is a bitch. It's perfectly acceptable, however, for women to be sad and dispirited.

So if you find yourself experiencing anger or withdrawal, chances are good something is scaring you. Now you only have to discover what it is.

> While fear is a powerful and sometimes complex emotion, unplugging from it is surprisingly straightforward.

Three things *not* to do as you embark on the expedition of discovering fear: 1. Try to change others (your fear is inside you). 2. Cope (you want to transform your fear, not accommodate it). 3. Try some superficial behavioral technique to avoid self-examination.

While fear is a powerful and sometimes complex emotion, unplugging from it is surprisingly straightforward. The following progression of simple practices have transformed the lives of many of my clients.

PRACTICES

Believe it or not, the first practice is to simply—

1. Breathe

FORTUNATELY, MOST OF THE TIME when we become physically scared, it was caused by an "error code" from the primitive part of the brain. These days, the briefest review of the situation usually reveals that killing someone or taking to our heels aren't the best responses. Recognizing that intellectually, however, doesn't free you from the grip of adrenaline. Breathing will.

Your lungs have several lobes. The bottom lobes sit directly atop your diaphragm. When something agitates or frightens you, take a deep breath, filling the bottom lobes first. Hold it. Slowly exhale. Do it again. Repeat one more time. Now, take a few more seconds and notice your body sensations. What's going on? Where are you holding tension?

Finally, can you name the emotions connected with those body sensations? They're there; you just have to look. This is how you become emotionally literate, and, again, it doesn't come naturally. (Often the emotion is anger, fear's favorite hideout.)

It takes about thirty seconds to breathe three good deep breaths, with a luxurious little pause after each one. Try it. How long does it take to identify body sensations and link them to emotions? Experiment on yourself by remembering a recent upset.

Then, Breathe, Feel, and Name that emotion. BFN is the acronym. The commandment is: Befriend thyself.

Please note: the purpose of this practice is not to dismiss the importance of whatever emotion is involved. The emotion is a signal. As with all signals (think traffic light), interpretation and response are everything.

Not to get too technical about it, but body sensations exist in a complex psychological fabric known as your "defensive routine." These subconscious behavioral reflexes are deeply woven into your life history. Your Jewish mother of a brain created them (without ever consulting you, of course). "Just trying to be helpful, dear."

But not only are these routines (habits) frequently unhelpful, they can be downright deadly, as in an emotional reaction that triggers a fatal event. Think asthma or heart attack. These tragedies happen all the time.

Those who get in the habit of regularly doing this simple breathing practice transform their lives in the most literal sense, because they actually remap their brains. They install new neural pathways. They recondition reflexes. They open new horizons of perception, expose otherwise hidden options, and recruit much more of their available intelligence.

In summary (and this is hardly original), breathing can save your life. But good breathing is only the beginning of real bravery and what it ushers into the world.

2. Tell Yourself a Story

Step 1: Name It

ONCE YOU'VE IDENTIFIED THE EMOTION, ask yourself where it's coming from. You'll have an answer before you're even finished forming the question. There's a technical term for your answer. It's called a story. You have a story about your emotional upset. So what is it? How are you "right" and the other "wrong"? Beyond the facts of the situation, what are your assessments that justify your emotions and behaviors?

This isn't a trick question, and it's not a setup. That story is very important. It has a truth all its own—a deep truth, with tendrils reaching back in time. So write down your story. Don't be shy, don't pull punches. Tell yourself this little tale of you. Lift it from the ether of your mind and put it on paper.

"A story is like water that you heat for your bath," said the Persian poet Rumi. "It carries messages between the fire and your skin. It lets them meet, and it cleans you!"

Step 2: Claim the Story

THIS IS SIMPLE, BUT NOT FACILE: just note where the story came from. It didn't come from the evening news, and you didn't read it in *The New York Times.* It came from you. Simply acknowledging that to yourself liberates you from the story's "reality" and creates a powerful possibility.

Neuroscience is bringing this kind of consciousness into focus as a synaptic event that is far more complex than reflexive thought. It appears to open the door for cognitive function—insight—that otherwise remains closed.

As cognitive neuroscientist Mark Jung-Beeman told *New Yorker* writer Jonah Lehrer for a July 28, 2008 article, insight happens when "executive-control areas" of the brain trigger a particular collaboration between the left and right hemispheres. Tiny, intense electrical storms "bind" neurons into new patterns that usher in new consciousness. The insight/epiphany/Eureka! instant is obviously one of the most spectacular moments in the human experience.

But so long as you think your story about an event is definitive, then your options are limited. Similarly, the moment you recognize the inherently incomplete nature of all stories, your options expand.

Step 3: Reframe Your Story

THIS IS EASIER SAID THAN DONE. Your story is for you what water is to a fish. It's a condition so basic that you don't even notice it, part of your unconscious bedrock, "the unregarded river" of your life, as Matthew Arnold put it.

But effectively reframing a story takes more than

intellectually spinning arbitrary alternative scenarios. You have to go deeper to find the emotional juice of other possibilities. This involves baiting your brain with sincere questions—the brain's a sucker for honest curiosity. It is honor-bound to serve you, but you must properly task it to get its most creative service.

Because so often fear and upset are intertwined with conflict, we'll offer several suggestions for reframing your story through empathy.

Simply ask yourself what others could be thinking such that their conduct makes sense to them. Simply saying to yourself, "I don't know what else is on their plate," deprives your story of its certainty. That lays the foundation for alternative stories that have the potential to sustain or restore relationship bonds and generate the results you want.

The key to empathy as a reframing tool is sincerity. Keep in mind this involves a soliloquy, a very private conversation between you and you in the privacy of your own mind. If you want your brain to provide you with credible explanations for the behavior of others, you have to be genuinely curious.

Obviously, this can be difficult. Empathy isn't about approving of the behavior of others. It's about understanding it, or trying to.

The human ego being what it is, the paradox of empathy is that it's toughest to access when it's needed most. The actions of others often scare, frustrate, anger, confuse and hurt us. That is to say, they "hook" us, releasing a synaptic trigger within us.

Because the absence of empathy always weakens or breaks relationships, which in turn wounds or kills teamwork and creativity, being able to reliably generate empathy in any situation is a useful skill that's well worth the effort of development.

Any time you find yourself in the midst of a conflict that makes the very idea of empathy galling, consider that in itself a signal that you need to interrupt your train of thought—defuse this synaptic bomb—and create empathy.

If that seems impossible, just remind yourself that empathy is part of your birthright. How else to explain that members of your species regularly risk, and sometimes forfeit, their lives to help strangers?

Another way to release empathy is to remember the good times. If you and the person with whom you're in conflict have shared special moments together, simply recall them in as much detail as possible. Call up the emotions you felt at those times. *Click*: you've re-established an emotional connection that goes beyond the current conflict. That may help you see it differently.

Yet another way to foster empathy is to create a story in your mind in which you cast your opponent as a sympathetic hero—imagining him or her saving someone from a frozen river, for instance. This is powerful, because all of us are ultimately sympathetic. None of us, to borrow from Matthew Arnold, really know the hills where our life rose, or the sea where it goes. We're all pilgrims trying to find our way.

Step 4: Re-aim Your Story

NOW THAT YOU'VE NAMED your emotions, you've reevaluated your own creation of a story surrounding the upset, and you're no longer assuming the worst about the person with whom you're in conflict, you are free to plan another conversation about the issue at hand. This is re-aiming. In this new re-aimed conversation, make a request or two. Ask for what you think will move the two of you forward. Then offer your own specific support to help your colleague meet that request. And, finally, secure a promise of action from your colleague. These requests, offers and promises are where the magic of re-aiming takes place. See if giving your colleague(s) the benefit of the doubt, along with the tangible requests, offers and secured promises, helps release the creativity and energy needed to achieve the results you're after.

CHAPTER FIVE

BE AUTHENTIC

The Momentary You and Why It Matters

*"This above all: to thine own self be true, and it must follow,
as the night the day, thou canst not then be false to any man."*

THAT WAS POLONIUS advising his son Laertes in *Hamlet*.
The old man was talking about the interpersonal value of
authenticity, which is one of the most important forms of
honesty. Being authentic, that is, being honest with yourself
about whether your actions reflect your values—or the values you espouse—makes you trustworthy.

Since Shakespeare put those
immortal words in Polonius' mouth
they have been a paradigm of excellent advice on all kinds of matters,
trustworthiness not least of all.

> Authenticity concentrates
> even the most confusing
> blur of events into a single
> point of focus: trust.

At the micro level, trustworthiness wins friends and
influences people. At the macro level, it creates healthy
economies, protecting savings, retirement nest eggs, college funds. Trustworthiness attracts bank depositors the way
honey attracts bees.

The tragedy of Polonius's advice is that it seems naïve—
what practical role has authenticity in a venal and complicated

world? This illusion of naïveté is tragic, because, over and over, from time immemorial, in every generation, experience proves that authenticity—the courage to be true to oneself—is the only thing that can ultimately make our personal lives and shared lives whole.

Authenticity is a wellspring of hope.

Besides, as everyone knows who has ever found themselves in urgent circumstances where leadership really mattered—where leadership had to be courageous, effective, and selfless—authenticity was unmistakably present. Authenticity concentrates even the most confusing blur of events into a single point of focus: trust.

And trust, neuroscience is showing, actually has a chemical basis. Just as endorphins relieve stress and suffuse us with a sense of wellbeing, trust also chemically inoculates us against anxiety while boosting confidence. Trust's chemical is the hormone oxytocin. Studies show that oxytocin facilitates the feeling of trust and measurably declines when trust breaks down.

As today's headlines show, when you remove trustworthiness from the marketplace you get results like the spectacle of auto giants, insurance giants, banking giants seeking taxpayer handouts. This is the equivalent of a prodigal Laertes blowing off the old man's advice—and then returning home with his tail between his legs, begging to be bailed out for his profligacy.

As you will soon see, evidence clearly suggests that epidemic inauthenticity played a major role in the creation of Wall Street's Monster and Detroit's breakdown.

The role inauthenticity played in the derivatives catastrophe is especially telling. Not without reason are derivatives referred to as "toxic." We all know that toxins can be devastating in infinitesimal concentrations. Take dioxin. So poisonous is it that its concentrations in the environment are measured in parts per trillion. One part per trillion is the equivalent of a single drop of water in three hundred Olympic swimming pools.

How many parts per trillion of authenticity on the part of America's banking and governmental leaders might have averted the global spread of the derivatives plague?

Evidence makes it clear that the answer would have been a tiny number. Consider Lebanon, until recently one of the world's quintessential failed states, and its central banker.

At a time when the world's biggest banks need taxpayer bailouts, Lebanon's banks have grown from $7 billion in assets in 1990 to $91 billion in 2009, according to a February 22, 2009 *Los Angeles Times* article. A major reason is that Riad Toufic Salame, governor of Lebanon's central bank, bucked the global tide and stubbornly regulated such structured investment products as derivatives. He prohibited Lebanon's banks from acquiring subprime mortgages. He was Horatius at the bridge, Hans Brinker with his finger in the dike. He kept toxic assets out of Lebanon's banking system.

Salame says he just never liked the way mysterious bundled debt instruments, like mortgage-backed securities, made him feel. What were they really worth? Who would pay them off? Such questions worried him. He refused to ignore his feelings.

At the heart of Lebanon's success, then, is Salame's authenticity. He explained that a deeply ingrained value shared by Lebanese and Middle Eastern bankers is that you don't loan money without knowing, as the *L.A. Times* reported, "who's going to pay you back." Derivatives, of course, made following such an ethic impossible.

"We could not really sense who would be responsible in the end to collect these loans," he said. "And we do not perceive banking as being a place to speculate on financial instruments that are not really concrete."

So instead of abandoning this value and going along with the global herd—and instead of bowing to pressure from Lebanese businessmen who wanted to cash in on the derivatives gusher that seemed to be soaking the rest of the world in wealth—Salame just said no.

Today, the world trusts Lebanon's bankers. Money is pouring into their banks. Lebanon is now being called "the Switzerland of the Middle East," a reference to pre-meltdown Swiss banks.

Meanwhile, China, America's largest debtor, questions whether America still deserves the trust to have the dollar serve as the "international reserve currency." Things might have been different if Alan Greenspan, or the U.S. Congress, had found the authenticity to act on the insight that Greenspan shared with Congress. Namely, "that derivatives could amplify crises."

Had that been the case, the words "The Federal Reserve, the central bank of the United States, provides the nation with a safe, flexible, and stable monetary system" might have meant something. Alas, inauthenticity made them hollow.

As a result, the contrast today between Alan Greenspan

and Riad Toufic Salame could not be greater. Salame's actions illustrate what real-world authenticity looks like.

Such evidence makes it clear why authenticity is essential to effective leadership. It's because trustworthiness is virtually synonymous with effective leadership. We don't wholly follow those we don't trust. Why should we? We may obey if we have no good alternative. But the difference between inspired and compelled performance is the difference between chalk and cheese.

Trustworthiness is virtually synonymous with effective leadership. We don't wholly follow those we don't trust.

When people are inspired, their imaginations fire, their life force quickens, they focus on a vision with the intensity needed to make it reality. Coerced performance, on the other hand—no matter how it is coerced—is just a form of forced labor. No leader pursuing optimum performance would settle for coercion were inspiration possible.

What do trustworthiness, and so authenticity, have to do with strong economies and healthy societies? As *Wall Street Journal* columnist Dennis K. Berman wrote in a November 25, 2008 commentary on curing mistrust in the financial system: "History shows that a nation can't have competition without trust and confidence."

Being true to yourself, or being authentic, requires developing the ability to notice, anywhere, under any circumstances, what you are feeling, thinking, believing, assuming to be true.

Being true to yourself, or being authentic, requires developing the ability to notice, anywhere, under any circumstances, what you are feeling, thinking, believing, assuming to be true. What, in other words, is your story about any particular situation?

Not only is this not the same thing as what has been called "positive thinking" by generations of self-help gurus, authenticity is often the opposite of positive thinking. Positive thinking can be self-delusional. It can be a form of habitual denial. Denial has no place in a conscious leader's repertoire.

I'm using "story" here not in the sense of conscious narrative, but in the neurological sense of perception. And perception, remember, is mostly nonconscious. That means the decision to become authentic is the decision to look for what is often not readily noticeable.

Learning to recognize that you have a story about every situation opens the door to noticing the unnoticed. This will change your life, and not figuratively. Reason: in the very moment that you observe yourself having an experience, instead of just having it as the creature of habit that you are, the character of that instant changes. And, at least for that one bright shining moment, you will know yourself as your life's storyteller instead of the unconscious central character in your life's story.

> And, at least for that one bright shining moment, you will know yourself as your life's storyteller instead of the unconscious central character in your life's story.

The more you string together such moments, the more access you will have to the awesome resources of adaptability, creativity, and insight with which you come fully equipped. The more adept you become at this process, the less you will feel like the plaything of forces beyond your control.

Nature gives us a clue about when to do this by offering a presenting condition: agitation.

Agitation is always a sign that consciousness is being called for. In the life of leaders, agitation may signal some stage of breakdown. Breakdowns call for breakthroughs, and they require awareness as a first step.

Authentic self-awareness is a good thing for anyone to practice, but for leaders it's critical. In the midst of any kind of agitation, the first step is to name the feeling behind the agitation. Are you angry, worried, frightened, suspicious, anxious, hurt? Whatever it is, give it that label. Nobody's watching. Nobody's listening. It's just you and this mystical data point called a feeling.

This isn't easy, as Daniel Goleman points out, because evolution has programmed you to not notice how you are noticing most of the time. Our culture, too, is often guilty of sabotaging self-awareness or consciousness. "Families, school, and churches provide us with little more than systematic training in self-estrangement and inauthenticity—a secular equivalent to The Fall," wrote Daniel Burston in his book, *The Crucible of Experience*.

The good news is that every single time you catch yourself in the act of noticing, you create a new synapse in your brain.

And so the lifelong habit of not noticing reinforces the habit. The longer the habit persists, the stronger it gets.

That's the bad news. Again, the good news is that every single time you catch yourself in the act of noticing, you create

> The first step toward authenticity is probably the hardest. It is to simply tell yourself the truth about what you're feeling. The reason this is hard is because two of the most powerful feelings in our emotional repertoire are fear and its next of kin, anger.

a new synapse in your brain. That remaps your brain one nano-increment at a time.

This is the miracle of neuroplasticity that, as the neuroscientists tell us, has the potential to actually change human nature.

The first step toward authenticity is probably the hardest. It is to simply tell yourself the truth about what you're feeling. The reason this is hard is because two of the most powerful feelings in our emotional repertoire are fear and its next of kin, anger.

Except in the case of adrenaline junkies or drama queens, most people try to avoid the unpleasantness of fear. This may be especially true of leaders, because of their mandate to role model courage. Who would want to follow a wobbly-kneed leader? But an actual perennial absence of fear (as opposed to a claimed or imagined absence of fear) would be a sign of either ignorance or mental disability. Fear is normal and inescapable in healthy, intelligent people. It's the healthy, intelligent management of it that doesn't come naturally. That's what takes intention and mastery.

If you think it's easy to identify your feelings, just ask yourself what you're feeling right now. Don't know? Close the book and sit with the question until the answer comes to you.

Chances are you weren't conscious of your feelings until you went looking for them. The exception, of course, would be if some overt event recently scared you or angered you, or made you happy enough to get your attention. Otherwise, why should you be sitting around contemplating the navel of your feelings?

Maybe the only feeling you were able to identify was irritation with the question about what you were feeling. If so, in the quest for emotional literacy that authenticity requires, that's good. Congratulations. You gave birth to a new synapse or two that will make answering the question easier next time you ask it. (And, if you take this chapter's advice, you will learn to ask yourself this question regularly.)

On the other hand, if you were diligent in your detective work, you might have been able to identify any number of feelings. Or remnants or braids or shadows or wisps of feelings. And, if you were patient with your emotional archeology, you might even have been able to surmise where the feelings came from. Or not. Sometimes our emotions simply baffle us, as synaptic ghosts of the forgotten past.

If you found lurking fear, anxiety or anger, it may have surprised you. If so, that illustrates Goleman's point about vital lies and self-deception. (If you didn't find such lurkers, however, you still can't be sure they're not there, safely tucked away in some cedar chest of the psyche.) This brings us to the point of personal emotional surveillance as it affects leaders.

In a sense, fear—emotion Numero Uno—is the business of leadership. Again, this is because leadership is about change, and our biologically programmed response to change ranges from irritation to fright, depending upon the magnitude of the change. How is society going to produce the energy, food, safe drinking water, healthcare and employment it needs, while protecting and cleansing the environment, raising sound children, and fighting all the wars—on drugs, crime, terrorists—and... and... and? Of course such questions might scare you. How they're answered could threaten your happiness, if not your survival.

Whether because of capitalism's relentless "creative destruction" (where every profitable innovation is displaced by another one), the competition for finite natural resources, or you name it, endless destabilization is a fact of life.

Continuously realigning human energy to respond to that challenge is leadership's job. Embedded in that task is an obstacle—the structure of the brain itself. The mandate for leaders is to harness their own fears, then to lead their followers *through* fear. In a sense, the workplace is the eternal valley of the shadow of fear. As many have been shocked to learn, it is not a setting where security can ever be guaranteed.

The mandate for leaders is to harness their own fears, then to lead their followers through fear.

An illuminating example of the high cost of inauthenticity emerges from the saga of the Sport Utility Vehicles (SUVs) from which the auto industry briefly made so much money. As author Malcolm Gladwell reported in a fascinating January 12, 2004 *New Yorker* article, "Big and Bad: How the SUV ran over automotive safety," Detroit always knew that it was catering to an illusion in selling the vehicles.

Detroit's own market research revealed the main reason consumers bought SUVs: they thought mass made them safer. On the contrary, as accident statistics proved, it made them and their passengers much more vulnerable to death and injury than they would be in normal cars. There were two reasons for this. First, SUVs were built on truck frames, which didn't have to meet the stringent safety standards of unit-body car construction. Second, they were much less maneuverable than cars, so avoiding accidents became far more difficult.

What made the enormous popularity of SUVs intriguing, as Detroit's marketers learned, was the disturbing psychological phenomenon of "learned helplessness."

As Gladwell reported, psychologists discovered it "from a series of animal experiments in the nineteen-sixties at the University of Pennsylvania. Dogs were restrained by a harness, so that they couldn't move, and then repeatedly subjected to a series of electrical shocks. Then the same dogs were shocked again, only this time they could easily escape by jumping over a low hurdle. But most of them didn't; they just huddled in the corner, no longer believing that there was anything they could do to influence their own fate. Learned helplessness is now thought to play a role in such phenomena as depression and the failure of battered women to leave their husbands, but one could easily apply it more widely. We live in an age, after all, that is strangely fixated on the idea of helplessness: we're fascinated by hurricanes and terrorist acts and epidemics like SARS [severe acute respiratory syndrome]—situations in which we feel powerless to affect our own destiny. In fact, the risks posed to life and limb by forces outside our control are dwarfed by the factors we can control…"

By working with French-born cultural anthropologist G. Clotaire Rapaille, a marketing consultant "whose specialty is getting beyond the rational," Detroit discovered that learned helplessness was an illusion originating in the primitive "reptilian" portion of the brain.

"And what Rapaille concluded from countless, intensive sessions with car buyers was that when SUV buyers thought about safety they were thinking about something that reached into their deepest unconscious," wrote Gladwell.

At some level these buyers feel that car accidents are inevitable and unavoidable, and the solution to that threat comes from the same subterranean level. " 'The No. 1 feeling is that everything surrounding you should be round and soft, and should give,' Rapaille told me. 'There should be air bags everywhere. Then there's this notion that you need to be up high. That's a contradiction, because the people who buy these SUVs know at the cortex level that if you are high there is more chance of a rollover. But at the reptilian level they think that if I am bigger and taller I'm safer. You feel secure because you are higher and dominate and look down. That you can look down is psychologically a very powerful notion. And what was the key element of safety when you were a child? It was that your mother fed you, and there was warm liquid. That's why cupholders are absolutely crucial for safety. If there is a car that has no cupholder, it is not safe. If I can put my coffee there, if I can have my food, if everything is round, if it's soft, and if I'm high, then I feel safe. It's amazing that intelligent, educated women will look at a car and the first thing they will look at is how many cupholders it has.'" Amazingly, these attitudes led Detroit's engineers to hold their SUV customers in contempt, wrote Gladwell:

> As Keith Bradsher writes in *High and Mighty*— perhaps the most important book about Detroit since Ralph Nader's *Unsafe at Any Speed*—what consumers said was, "If the vehicle is up high, it's easier to see if something is hiding underneath or lurking behind it." Bradsher brilliantly captures the mixture of bafflement and contempt that many auto executives feel toward the customers who buy their SUVs. Fred J. Schaafsma, a top engineer for General Motors, says, "Sport-utility owners tend to be more like, 'I wonder how people view me,' and are more willing to trade off flexibility or functionality to get that." According to Bradsher, internal industry market research concluded that SUVs tend to be bought by people who are insecure, vain, self-centered, and self-absorbed, who are frequently nervous about their marriages, and who lack confidence in their driving skills. Ford's SUV designers took their cues from seeing "fashionably dressed women wearing hiking boots or even work boots while walking through expensive malls." Toyota's top marketing executive in the United States, Bradsher writes, loves to tell the story of how at a focus group in Los Angeles "an elegant woman in the group said that she needed her full-sized Lexus LX 470 to drive up over the curb and onto lawns to park at large parties in Beverly Hills." One of Ford's senior marketing executives was even blunter: "The only time those SUVs are going to be off-road is when they miss the driveway at 3 a.m."

Famously, but briefly, SUVs yielded historic Detroit profitability. Because they were cheaper to build than cars, their profit margins were dramatically higher. Not only was Ford's truck plant in Wayne, Michigan, where giant Expeditions were built, the most profitable of Ford's fifty-three assembly facilities, as Gladwell wrote: "By the late nineteen-nineties, it had become the most profitable factory of any industry in the world. In 1998, the Michigan Truck Plant grossed eleven billion dollars, almost as much as McDonald's made that year. Profits were $3.7 billion. Some factory workers, with overtime, were making two hundred thousand dollars a year."

A decade later, Ford CEO Alan Mulally appeared before Congress, along with the CEOs of GM and Chrysler, seeking a taxpayer bailout. In a sense, this was eloquent testimony about the unaffordable cost of inauthenticity. The inauthenticity was shared by Detroit and its customers.

How likely is it that Detroit's engineers and leaders were facing the truth of how they felt about selling SUVs? Even with the prodigious profits, bonuses, and salaries to balm the cognitive dissonance, is it conceivable that they could have been marketing to the reptilian brains of their customers without having some pang of, if not outright discomfort, at least doubt? And the customers themselves—given their demographics, was it really conceivable that they were unaware of their irrational buying decisions?

When a smaller car collides with an SUV, it is so deadly one might conclude that SUV owners have contempt for everybody else on the road. Bradsher wrote that SUVs appeal to "Americans' most selfish and even vicious instincts…."

Please note: this is not an issue of morality. It's not about right and wrong. It's merely about awareness. Whatever feelings Detroit and its SUV customers might have had about the products, those feelings were sources of information, data points to be considered. Let's say, in both the case of the auto executives and their customers, they were haunted by doubt (the way the NASA engineers were about the O-rings). That doubt presented an opportunity to shift to decisions and actions in keeping with the voice of conscience—and consciousness.

As things turned out, inauthenticity was the insuperable hidden cost that figures in the decline, if not ultimately the demise, of the American automobile industry.

It is now inarguable that rampant inauthenticity played a similar role in the global financial crisis, its fingerprints smeared all over the economic crash of 2008.

That doubt presented an opportunity to shift to decisions and actions in keeping with the voice of conscience—and consciousness.

"Toxic Assets Were Hidden Assets," Hernando de Soto wrote in the March 25, 2009, *Wall Street Journal*. The result, he noted, was a massive breakdown of trust in the financial system. Such a breakdown, he explained, "sets off a chain reaction, paralyzing credit and investment, which shrinks transactions and leads to a catastrophic drop in employment and in the value of everyone's property."

Where were Horatius or Riad Toufic Salame when we needed them?

"Property is much more than a body of norms," wrote de Soto. "It is also a huge information system that processes raw data until it is transformed into facts that can be tested for truth, and thereby destroys the main catalysts of recessions and panics—ambiguity and opacity."

Derivatives, as they were sold to the investing public for the past two decades, contained an inherent untruthfulness: nobody could tell what they were worth.

Had the sellers of derivatives simply said to their customers: "We have no idea what these things are worth," their sales may well have come to a crashing halt. And yet that was the truth that nobody uttered.

As the massive derivatives deceit spread through the global economy, it is simply inconceivable that there weren't untold trillions of moments of inauthenticity on the parts of sellers. Would that old Polonius had been whispering in their ears: *"To thine own self be true."*

They couldn't have done that—been true to themselves—and sold derivatives, too. At least not enough of them to do much damage.

Put differently, imagine the difference a few parts per trillion of Lebanese banker authenticity would have made on Wall Street. Clearly, the derivatives catastrophe might well have been prevented if the leaders of the free world had asked a simple question. No matter that the question may sound as naïve today as it did in Polonius's time. We ignore it at our peril. The question is …

PRACTICES

1. Where Am I Honestly Stuck?

Step 1.

IDENTIFY TWO OR THREE challenging relationships, pending decisions, or issues you're stuck on. (Those in which you are not being authentic, such as withholding disclosure about your concerns/feelings/ fears.)

- Pick one and write out the story about it. What are you holding back? Explain why. Be specific about your fears or concerns. Make the story as explicit as possible. Now recognize yourself, not the events, as the story's author.

- Identify the key value or principle that you have, inadvertently or not, been ignoring.

- Once that narrative is clear, decide if you need to talk frankly with the other(s) involved in the dilemma. (Why would you do that? What significant purpose would it serve? Be clear. What would matter most to you about solving this dilemma? Let yourself bask in the imagined feeling of a solution.) What you want to do is review, in detail, your concerns and the concerns of other(s) involved. Then make requests and/or offers that move you and the other(s) onto new pathways toward new results.

Step 2.
ASK, "WHAT'S AN IDEAL SOLUTION?"

- Forget that the conflicted/challenged relationship involves you. Merely ask yourself what the optimum response would look like.

- List the components of this optimum response as though it didn't involve you. This lets you look beyond your perceived limitations and your fears. It lets you ask whether you would be willing to attempt to grow, to cultivate new skills in order to rise to the occasion.

- Use the larger purpose you identified in Step 1 as a motive for incrementally incorporating these preferred actions into your own performance.

2. Be "Complete" with "Incompletion"

"COMPLETION" IS A SPECIFIC PSYCHOLOGICAL state where even though the object of my distress or conflict isn't resolved or finished I can be okay with it. "Unfinished" or "unsolved" doesn't have to necessarily mean that I am upset.

Being complete with something "unfinished" allows me to just hold it until my conscious or unconscious mind can solve it. Declaring oneself complete with a really important unsolved problem is the epitome of "having" one's mind.

Obviously, following the Polonian path—being true to yourself—isn't always easy. That means it's often not possible to reconcile conflict within ourselves. Auto executives with qualms about SUVs, or bank leaders made sleepless over derivatives, are just two real-world examples. The list of others is infinite. When faced with internal conflicts like these, we move away from authenticity when we deny them. It is truer to simply acknowledge to ourselves that the conflicts exist.

Step 1.
MAKE A LIST of any such current conflicts or unsolved problems you have. Pick one to work on.

Step 2.
NOTICE THE TENSION you feel surrounding this conflict or unsolved problem, and then let it go. Breathe. Right now relax into being complete. It's okay. Trust that resolution will come, and that your trust in yourself about this will reward you with a little dose of oxytocin. And that oxytocin will be shared by others. That, of course, isn't a "solution," but self-trust, and trust inspired in others, makes a solution much more likely.

CHAPTER SIX

BE BRILLIANTLY INTENTIONAL

**The beacon within can cut through any darkness.
Here's how to use it…**

෴

*"It has been said that the great events of the world
take place in the brain. It is in the brain, and the brain only,
that the great sins of the world take place also."*
—OSCAR WILDE

BY NOW YOU KNOW that almost all of our perceptions take on a form of storytelling. It's the way our brains process the conscious and non-conscious input of our senses. And that input, as we have also seen, comes to us through the synaptic filter, the "story editor" if you will, automatically installed as a free peripheral by the act of living.

So synapses form the clockwork organism of habit. They are the "structure" in the structural determinism discussed in Chapter Two. I think you could say that we are our synapses packaged in skin, bone and muscle. The twinkling impulses of those synapses propel our habits. They move us in every sense.

> Habits are the key. Our experience creates them. Habits return the favor by shaping our experience.

We come, then, to an important insight about the curiously circular nature of the human condition: life shapes thought; thought shapes life. Habits are the key. Our experience creates them. Habits return the favor by shaping our experience.

Habits, to repeat a mantra I constantly use with my clients, aren't bad—except when they are. Something Dr. Joshua Berke, a University of Michigan neuroscientist, says about habits strikes me as profoundly important to all leaders in our quicksilver world. Dr. Kessler quotes Berke in *The End of Overeating* this way:

"'A habit is a way of saving cognitive effort. It makes sense to have a system that, when faced with the same situation over and over, allows a fixed response without having to think about it.'

"Habits are learned slowly, but once they are in place, they are by their very nature difficult to break. 'One defining feature of habits is that they are resistant to extinction,' said Berke. 'Habits are very inflexible…. They're very unresponsive when a situation changes.'"

When I think of the speed at which technology is changing our "situation," that last observation of Dr. Berke really gets my attention. Many scientists studying global climate change, for instance, talk of dangerous anthropogenic interference (DAI) with the earth's climate. This human interference, they warn, now threatens humans with catastrophe. Manmade catastrophe has already hit the manmade global economy.

But where do these catastrophes actually come from? Because we don't intentionally create them, it logically follows that they are "accidents." I think of them as "synaptic accidents." I suspect that they're caused by unconscious habits of thought that lead us to behave in ways that don't meet our needs in the end—that cause us to miss the mark. These particular habits, then—the ones implicated in what I'm calling synaptic accidents—would fall under the category of "bad habits." "Habits that hinder" is how I usually talk about them with my clients.

Synaptic accidents, these innocent mistakes, are like an error code in the brain, leading to spectacular mistakes of perception. One could argue that weapons of mass destruction, financial and otherwise, represent such perceptual mistakes. By comparison, attacking Mack trucks mistaken for bears appears positively reasonable. In any case, the character of synaptic accidents seems like a kind of sin in the original sense of the word.

The generic word for sin in Biblical Hebrew, *het*, means simply to err, to miss the mark. It wasn't about moral infraction. In New Testament classical Greek, the word *hamartia* is usually translated as sin, and it, too, means to "miss the mark." In Old English archery the identical word—hamartia—meant the same, missing the target or missing the mark.

Missing the mark means simply not doing what you intended, or doing something you didn't intend.

At the risk of being repetitive, I'll note that the White House, Congress, and Wall Street (collectively, one of the biggest brain trusts around) all missed the mark on the "weapons of financial mass destruction" known as derivatives. That means that those who offered leadership about hitting the mark on this important matter—Warren Buffett, Brooksley Born, the General Accounting Office—also missed the mark. That is, they failed to lead, because their offers of leadership were rejected.

I accept the risk of repetition here, because the evidence is clear that our synaptic accidents—our sins of missing the mark—are getting more frequent and more severe. The evidence is just as clear—to me, anyway—that unless we do something to stop it, this trend is likely to continue until we melt down something that's harder to fix than the economy. That the stakes of leadership have become so high is the whole point of this book.

The evidence is clear that our synaptic accidents—our sins of missing the mark—are getting more frequent and more severe.

Because all life is just a story, let's make one up to show how what I call "brilliant intentionality" can help us hit the mark—accomplish what we intend—by snapping us out of the neural hypnosis of habit. We'll take a hypothetical executive in the banking industry, a man hired two years before the economic meltdown. Our fictional hero is a respected financier, sharp as a tack, honest as the day is long. A regular Jack Bogle/ Warren Buffett kind of guy. We'll call him J.D.

J.D.'s close friend, Fred, chairman of the board of an investment bank, persuades J.D. to become the bank's new CEO, giving assurances that this particular bank has relatively little exposure to the now-controversial mortgage-backed securities. J.D. didn't just fall off the turnip wagon, so he does a little due diligence and finds no evidence that Fred was wrong.

J.D. begins work and is immediately alarmed to discover that the chairman wasn't just wrong; he was practically deluded. J.D. issues a detailed report to the board, outlining radical corrective steps, calling for an immediate meeting to discuss the situation. However, both the report and meeting request are greeted by deafening silence. J.D.'s old friend, the chairman, will not return his calls. J.D. is in a state of shock. He understands that if the company were to be engulfed by worthless debts, it could escalate to unthinkable proportions.

"Can you say 'global financial crisis?'" he ends the report.

It's been more than a week since J.D. had a good night's sleep, which is completely unlike him. His wife is worrying about his health.

J.D.'s first step in bringing consciousness to bear on his situation is to name his story by clarifying his thoughts and feelings. He pulls out a notepad and writes:

"I'm very, very angry. I can't believe it, but I'm afraid Fred has set me up. It's outrageous for him and the board to have lured me into this situation and then abandon me to it. Do they mean to make me a scapegoat? It's possible this company has engaged in fraud. Is Fred part of it? Is the entire board? Or has my memo terrified them by introducing them to facts they should have known long ago? Even if the board itself is not criminally culpable, it has done an inexcusable job of protecting stakeholders… I owe a duty to this board, yes, but I have an even greater duty to the truth…."

Steam billowing from his ears, J.D. fills four handwritten legal pages just like that. It's a devastating indictment of his colleagues, and of the government regulatory system that allowed this crisis to develop. The story also is a frank confession of J.D.'s own fear. That's the critical point of this example. J.D.'s fear is a synaptic event.

After his journaling session, for some reason, J.D. sleeps better that night. (If J.D. were real, were he actually one of my clients, I would say that he slept better because, with his journaling, he actually *made* a new story. No longer is he just an upset man. Now he is an observer, a man writing about his upset. That is a different man.)

But J.D. still has a problem. What to do?

So he calls his coach—*moi.*

Now, J.D. has already undertaken a sophisticated self-examination by telling himself his story of what's happening to him. Being able do that under stress is the first step toward the kind of radical creativity demanded by the major challenges we face today. A powerful second step is becoming intentional within the context of that story. This is what I mean by "brilliant" intentionality—brilliant in the sense of shining the light of consciousness on one's own thought processes.

Simply asking yourself the question "What do *I* want to have happen?" in the midst of events that are already happening creates possibilities that transcend your first synaptic response.

It shifts you from being an actor in the world's drama to being the playwright of your own experience within that drama. And that, of course, changes the drama around you. Make no mistake: that's a revolution in the sovereign country of your psyche.

Brilliant intentionality, then—as opposed to unchecked synaptic response to perceived threat—involves disarming your own psychological defenses by naming and claiming your story. And believe me, "disarm" is the right word.

I consider our psychological defenses to be hair trigger neural structures that suffuse us. Again, genetic inheritance and life experience unavoidably install them. Although these structures express themselves through measurable physical events, they don't exist themselves as physical things that a surgeon could remove. They are psychological structures. They are smoke. Here's how I think they work. Some event or thought trips one of these triggers. Emotions are released. Behavior begins. What happens next is called life. It's called history.

The simple act of naming a story—"I'm mad, scared, offended, etc."—then claiming the story as your own, recognizing that it is an internal, not an external thing, disarms the trigger. That buys you precious moments in which to choose what action to take. In these instants, the direction of one's life can change. So can history itself.

In the land of your psyche, in which you are monarch, that's a revolution.

The possibilities of revolutionary new action that result from this intimate emotional disarmament are unique to you. And they are almost infinite. They reflect the story of events as you *choose* to tell the story, one that now reflects your own goals and values. This new story is, in the cognitive sense, *brilliant*.

Remember, *all* of our behavior has a single underlying purpose: survival. That means, in the neuronal canyons of your mind, a chorus is always singing. Call it the "Don't Die Chorus."

Sometimes it merely whispers, a wind in the willows. Sometimes it howls like a storm at sea. But it's always there—in your mind and the minds of everyone around you. "Don't die," go the lyrics in the windmills of humanity's mind. "Don't die, don't die, don't die."

To fully appreciate what this means, try setting the words "don't die" to a tune in your mind right now.

Try something energizing, like the William Tell Overture (The theme from The Lone Ranger TV show, for those old enough to remember): *"Don't die ba—da-bump-bump-bump; don't die ba-da-bump-bump-bump..."*

Or something grand—the chorus, say, in the fourth movement of Beethoven's 9th. *"Dough-ohhhh-oh-ohho-ohohohooo-ohhoooo-ohhoooh-oh-oh-oh-oh-oh-oh DON'T DIE!..."*

Or an infant's song: Lullaby and Good Night: *"Don't die, and don't die, and don't die, and don't die..."*

Because unmanaged defensive routines are rooted in fear, they often drain energy and harm productivity by making us "play small," focusing on self-protection.

There. You just laid down a little synaptic track that echoes the all-time No. 1 hit that's been playing in every human brain for as long as human brains have been around. Humanity marches to this little ditty with greater gusto than ever it did to any military air. It has us on constant alert, ready to launch into a defensive routine.

A defensive routine is a synaptic accident waiting to happen.

Obviously, unmanaged defensive routines can be costly. At the personal level, they can feel lonely and scary. They *are* lonely, because they cut us off from ourselves and others, often causing us to act in ways we're not proud of. And they're doubly scary, because we're not consciously in control while in the reflexive grip of a defensive routine. We are, in such moments, actually neurologically crippled by our habits.

Moreover, because unmanaged defensive routines are rooted in fear, they often drain energy and harm productivity. It goes without saying that they wreck creativity and deep reflection by making us "play small," focusing on self-protection.

Every time we triumph over a defensive routine, what my colleague Mark Shunk calls the angel in the stone has just been freed a little bit more.

Insight into my clients' defensive routines is fundamental in my approach to coaching, because I need to be able to see not just the world my clients see—that is, objective, measurable data like revenue, market share, etc.—but also the lens through which they see it.

Over the years, I have found that most of our defensive routines stem from four classical fears. These fears are "normal," which is to say I believe we all experience them in some combination or degree of intensity. Based on the way life has molded us, most of us appear to be especially afraid of being seen as one of the following:

- Stupid / Foolish / Idiotic

- A Pretender / A Fraud

- An Outcast / Rejected / Unlovable

- Powerless / Weak / Ineffective

Let me repeat. *All* of us experience these fears. That means the best, brightest and most blessed among us have to wrestle with them. Reduced to words on a page, they may seem harmless, but they aren't. This is because they often magnify, distort, and obscure the everyday events of life so much as to become saboteurs of the "normal" psyche. At the very least they cause needless suffering. At their worst they make life a living hell. They turn human affairs into a minefield.

I have known defensive routines to derail the most promising careers, destroy good marriages, ruin lives. How? They have a nasty habit of triggering a million forms of subtle, chronic fight-or-flight behavior when fighting or fleeing aren't the best moves.

For the most part, my clients retain my colleagues and me because they recognize that only by taking full responsibility for their defensive routines can they reduce the frequency of being run by them. That allows them to call forth more of their gifts. As they experience that, they quickly recognize that even though building the muscle called "awareness" takes some small discipline, the dividends dwarf the effort. It helps keep them from taking their mistakes so hard. It also helps them guide others away from their own defensive routines. That helps lead everyone around the minefield.

I can imagine a coaching conversation with J.D. going something like this:

J.D. As you can see from my correspondence to the board, this company faces a very serious problem. And I am at a complete loss to understand the board's silence. Neither the chairman nor any of the other directors have responded to my report or my several follow-up e-mails and phone calls. Obviously, I can't lead this company without complete board support.

Michael O'Brien. Clearly not. Your problem is that, through your report, you have offered the board leadership. So far, the board is choosing not to follow you. Ergo, you have failed to lead them. So the first thing you have to ask yourself is if you want to make another offer of leadership. You have to choose. No one can choose for you. Do you still want to try to lead this board?

J.D. Are you asking me that now?

M.O'B. Yes.

J.D. (Silence.)

M.O'B. Right. It's a difficult question. And it's not about right and wrong. You could resign right now and no one would blame you. I wouldn't blame you. You could go play golf. You don't need this. Moreover, based on what I know of your reputation, and based on your findings, I would almost expect you to resign at this point. So why wouldn't you?

J.D. Are you being rhetorical or really asking?

M.O'B. Really asking.

J.D. (Long pause.) Of course I can hit the chute. Of course I can leave. That's not my preference, however. I do want to lead, I just don't know how to, under these circumstances. I can't *make* these people follow me. You read my report. You see the evidence that my board doesn't want to face facts. I don't know what to do!

M.O'B. Got it. You chose to offer leadership. Your board rejected your offer. Now you have to choose again. So again I ask you: why would you want to lead this organization under these circumstances?

J.D. (Another long pause.) Well, for one thing, I believe that the success of this company is very important to a whole bunch of people, beginning with its shareholders and stakeholders. But it doesn't stop there. If this company goes down in flames, it's going to spread to the economy. Innocent people will suffer. That engages me. I really love to take care of people's money. That's what Fred and the board asked me to do. So that's number one. Number two: this is an extremely interesting situation. The way scientists are fascinated with Ebola virus—set aside the human drama—this situation fascinates me. I've spent my life in finance, and this is one of the most intriguing problems I've ever seen! I'd love to be part of the solution…

M.O'B. Let me stop you right there. You've just given me two good reasons why you'd like to lead this company. One is of the heart. Taking care of people's money in high integrity ways is sacred to you. I get chills hearing you talk about it. This is beyond skills and abilities. This is something that you care deeply about. The other reason is of the head. This is endlessly fascinating to you. It's a huge problem. And you think you can fix it. Good. Thank you. You've convinced me. Have you convinced yourself?

J.D. Absolutely!

M.O'B. So, if you choose to lead, these are two reasons why you would. So now you have to choose. Do you still want to lead this company?

J.D. (Silence.)

M.O'B. Obviously you can't lead your management team without first leading your board. And your board seems to have rejected your leadership. So how can you get your board's support?

J.D. (Silence. Frown.)

(N.B.: a frown is actually a sign of strain. I'm pretty sure about where the frown is coming from. I suspect that my client is straining against the synaptic structure of a powerful defensive routine. I have a hypothesis about his struggle, but I need him to speak before I'll know if it's accurate. I'm pleased that he doesn't attempt a knee-jerk response; this is heavy lifting. I let him struggle with his discomfort for a moment.)

M.O'B. This is where intentionality comes in. What do you intend to create that you would choose to lead the board members toward? Notwithstanding the reasons for their silence so far—which are probably all fear-based—where would you lead the board right now? What would it look like for this board to behave as you want it to?

J.D. First it would set aside its own self-interest. This board has a fiduciary duty—which it accepted!—to read my report, think about it, and convene the meeting I requested, so that we can initiate the strategy necessary to deal with this problem. And they're not doing that. So, the first thing I would do is give them the opportunity to rethink their inaction, to get clear individually and collectively about their responsibility. So I guess my first intention would be to help them face their dilemma. The problem is, I don't know what their dilemma is. I don't know if they feel caught up in something that's beyond them. I don't know if they're afraid of legal exposure. I just don't know.

M.O'B. How could you find out?

J.D. Well… (another pause.) Well… (sigh) I could send them another memo. Tell 'em again that I have to meet with them. Give 'em a deadline this time. In other words, I could demand action from them in time certain to enable me to take the action I hired on to take. I could inform them that without that, as much as I would like to serve them and this company, I will be unable to do so. I will have to resign.

This suggests to me that my hypothesis was correct. That J.D. can think of only two options—ultimatum (fight), or resignation (flight)—bears the earmarks of a classic defensive routine.

Again, this routine results from years of neuronal sculpting by the potent chemicals known as neurotransmitters. Neurologically, this is where all habits come from, good and bad. The whole point of understanding defensive routines is that the neural circuitry of a bad habit can be circumvented by the circuitry of a good habit. This is done in part through the use of goals and intentions, and it takes serious effort.

In J.D. I am dealing with a man of high intelligence,

integrity, passion, and action. I know his type well. J.D.'s defensive routine is a familiar one: he does not suffer fools. J.D. banishes fools from his kingdom (a fight response), or he flees and starts a new kingdom (flight). Deep down, J.D. fears being seen as a fool. And right now he doesn't know how to disarm his triggered aversion to ignorance or deceit by applying his acknowledged wish and declared intention to help his board rise to the challenge before it.

M.O'B. Okay, I'm going to say what you said differently. You could threaten them. You could threaten them with what you know how to do well, which is leave and go off and do your own thing. But I just heard you tell me why your preference is to lead these people. So how well do you think your threat will work?

J.D. I have no idea. I'm truly flummoxed...

M.O'B. Well, let me hazard a guess. Given that these are all highly successful people, my hunch is they're fearful of looking wrong, bad, or stupid. That, of course, could be linked to the fear of being made to appear negligent, which could easily link to anxieties about failing their fiduciary duties. My guess is that a threat will not ease their fears and move them into positive action. It's easy for me to believe that your report shocked them.

J.D. I'd bet on it.

M.O'B. My guess is that your report, while it wasn't your intention, has already threatened them. So more threats aren't likely to be effective. I'm not saying that leading by threat is bad, or should be off the table, just that you've already done it, however accidentally...

We'll stop there; to take this scenario further risks making J.D. a straw man, and his dilemma is as relevant as it gets.

It's the same basic problem that leaders always face. Namely, getting people to go in a new direction.

J.D.'s challenge, in fact, is merely a variation on the leader's basic task, which is to continuously create new possibilities out of thin air. Beyond the particulars of J.D.'s hypothetical problem, it's the same basic problem that leaders always face. Namely, getting people to go in a new direction. Every time you do that you are faced with the innumerable fears of those whom you would lead.

You cannot lead people in a new direction without leading them through their defensive routines. That puts you in the middle of a human minefield. The only way to successfully negotiate that minefield is to first deal with your own defensive routines. If ever there was a time in which one must first lead by example, this is it.

I certainly don't know what J.D. "should" do. Again, Shoulds tend to emerge from the nautilus of our habits and conditioning, from the hall of mirrors of our stories. Coulds are found in a more exotic landscape. That is the frontier into which I would attempt to guide J.D., steering by the compass of his own declared values and goals—his brilliant intentionality.

In an actual coaching session, I would want to help J.D. identify as many things as possible that he could do to act on his intentions. It's a highly personal strategy. J.D. himself needs to embrace the options of the various steps he could take to serve the intention that is the organic expression of his own goals and values. These are not duties embedded in his job description. In fact, they are not duties at all. They are possibilities that flow from his authentic self. As Mark Shunk might say, we are now in angel-in-the-stone territory.

That J.D. might at first be unconscious of exciting new possibilities matters not at all. For J.D., I'm confident in saying, many such possibilities are discoverable. I can almost guarantee that a long list of possible Coulds—action steps— would be uncovered because of the intensity of J.D.'s desire.

This is the emotional key to radical creativity—to brilliant intentionality—that many people don't understand. If you don't care about something, you can't act as though you do and expect your mind to believe you and generate high-octane creativity. (By the way, the high-octane chemical involved here is the very neurotransmitter, dopamine, that caused Pavlov's dog to drool. Dopamine fuels reward-seeking behavior. You can administer it to yourself with meaningful goals that stimulate powerful actions.) You can't fake caring. You can't hide from the truth. And you can't force it on others, either.

> **If you don't care about something, you can't act as though you do and expect your mind to believe you and generate high-octane creativity.**

J.D. knows that he cares. What he doesn't know is if or how much or why his board members care. If he's just going to throw in the towel, that doesn't matter. If he wants to at least try to lead them, it matters a great deal.

So J.D. has to find out what's going on with that board. His first Coulds all have to revolve around making contact with the directors and finding out what's going on with them. His preliminary list of options might include:

He could arrive unannounced at their offices. He could ring their home doorbells; lob pebbles at their bedroom windows; ambush them on the links. He could try to make contact through mutual friends or other third parties.

The greater J.D.'s sense of moral duty, the more forceful the options he might consider. Thus, he could have corporate legal "summon" the board to meet. He could fire a shot across the board's bow by providing his report to the Federal Reserve Board or the SEC. He could leak it to the press. He could present it to the media outright in an open press conference. Whatever actions J.D. takes that are aligned with his brilliant intentions, every time he takes them he will reward himself with a little shot of dopamine. In this way the circuitry of a new habit, a brilliantly intentional one, will be wired.

Again, J.D. can always just resign. But to the extent that he perceives real peril for innocent parties, and believes that he can do something about it, and *wants* to do something about it, he will likely view resignation as a last resort. How he views his duty will shape both the justification and inspiration of the leadership he will choose to offer.

And the intensity of his intention—the *brilliance* of it—will be his own lodestar. It doesn't guarantee that he will succeed. It does ensure that he will act in a way he considers uniquely appropriate. And the neurological reward of his effort is certain.

The simple reality is that J.D. cannot lead without first offering to lead and having the offer accepted. If there is no offer, or if there is no acceptance of an offer, clearly there can be no leadership.

Assuming J.D.'s next offer of leadership is made and accepted, his subsequent steps, as I see them, are relatively straightforward.

He needs to ascertain the board members' own stories about the company's circumstances; he needs to know their reaction to his report, and how they see their own responsibilities as a result of its findings; he needs to understand what, if anything, is causing them to freeze up.

Equipped with that information, and not encumbered by his own fears and defensive routine, J.D. is now ready to go to work as a leader. That means leading people through the valley of the shadow of defensive routines (which actually is the valley of the shadow of death) toward a shining vision of something truly new and wonderful.

Said differently, the leader's real business is hope. Psychologists equate hope with optimism. And optimism, as Martin Seligman and the positive psychology movement are teaching us, is the body's own wonder drug. In a sense, that makes great leaders the world's most important pharmacists.

> That means leading people through the valley of the shadow of defensive routines toward a shining vision of something truly new and wonderful.

Pragmatically, J.D.'s next steps are to enroll his directors in his vision of the company's future and to facilitate them in identifying their own intentions in supporting the pursuit of that vision. That done, J.D. will be ready to repeat the same process with his management team. Of such stardust are turnarounds made.

Before getting to this point, J.D. will have negotiated some of his own defensive routines, and helped his board negotiate some of theirs.

Put another way, in acting on his brilliant intention, J.D. will have overcome the siren song of his and others' Don't Die Chorus.

E.B. White once wrote of "man's fantastic battle with himself." What that's really about, I believe, is our defensive routines.

In his book, *You Are What You Say*, Dr. Matthew Budd offers a poignant example of how defensive routines—triggered fears—operate in our lives with painful, and sometimes even fatal, results. At a workshop Dr. Budd was attending, an obnoxious trainer was barking ground rules when one of the participants at his table began having a coughing fit. Given his medical training, Dr. Budd soon realized she was having an asthma attack.

"Asthma is a condition in which the air passages go into spasm and a person's breathing becomes difficult," Budd wrote. "An asthma attack can be serious, even fatal."

The woman's coughing grew so severe that Budd was about to assist her. "My mind was racing," Budd continued. "Maybe she ate something for breakfast that she was allergic to, or maybe it's the paint or rugs in this hall, or maybe there's a fungus in the air-conditioning system."

Just as Budd rose to help, the woman leaped up herself and angrily wheezed a protest to the trainer: "Don't tell me what to do," is all she could say before violent coughing stopped her.

"Did you hear the ground rules?" said the trainer. "No talking until you're called on! I didn't call on you."

By then Budd was at the woman's side. "This woman is having an asthma attack," he told the trainer. The trainer waved him away, got right in the woman's face, and said, "Look at me, I am not your father!"

Wrote Budd: "When I heard this, I was sure that he was crazy."

The woman's fury increased; her coughing seemed about to strangle her. Dr. Budd's Hippocratic oath had him on the verge of ordering the trainer to back off. But the trainer's voice dropped, and he quietly told the woman to look at his right ear. The woman complied.

"It's not your father's ear, is it?" asked the workshop leader.

"No, of course not."

The strange dialogue continued, addressing the trainer's nose, eyes, mouth and head. The trainer's voice softened into compassion. "I'm not your father, am I? So why are you so angry? Just raise your hand and wait to be called on before you speak."

"No, you're not my father, but it feels that way," answered the woman. She relaxed, but she was sobbing bitterly, "a whole body cry, not a polite sob," wrote Dr. Budd. That moment changed Budd's life as a physician. He had seen something his medical training had not exposed him to. He saw a human trigger pulled, and then relaxed.

"Now it was me gasping," he wrote. "I had seen something that completely upset my worldview. I believed that asthma is a disease caused by the body's response to a substance to which it is allergic. Every first-year medical student knows this."

He explained that if he had merely heard the event described, "I would have been amused and very skeptical. But I didn't hear or read about it, *I had seen it with my own eyes.* Her attack had cleared up without the aid of inhaled or intravenous medications, the usual treatments for asthma."

The best leadership can be seen as a living art form. Great leaders are more like sculptors, or maybe even chefs, than anything else.

The voice of a skilled leader had been used as medicine.

In a somewhat less dramatic but equally transformative manner, J.D. can address fears in his workplace.

This book's point of view is that the best leadership can be seen as a living art form. Great leaders are more like sculptors, or maybe even chefs, than anything else. Their medium is neurons. From the raw material of the psyche, from the tangled narrative of history and the jumble it makes of the human condition at the level of neurons, leaders are charged to create their own installment of humanity's story. To do that, they must begin at the beginning, with their own autobiographies.

Here are several proven practices that will help.

PRACTICES

1. Wake Up to Your Defensive Routines

JUST AS OUR CHARACTER J.D. had a defensive routine that prevented him from offering leadership at a time when it was most needed, all of us frequently react defensively when we feel threatened.

Bring to mind a current conflict, major upset or breakdown you have. In your journal briefly summarize: Who are you upset with? What's the conflict about? Why is this important to you? Now review the common *Fight* and *Flight* behaviors listed below. Check off the top two or three that you are using in your selected situation.

When threatened, I typically *Fight* by:

☐ Raising my voice louder than others – shouting them down.

☐ Using absolute statements like "The fact is…" or "It's obvious that…"

☐ Interrogating others to trap them into surrender.

☐ Taking a "snapshot" view of situations and quickly deducing the motives of others.

☐ Labeling and judging others based on my views.

☐ Using "evidence" to prove my views are better than the other person's views.

- ☐ Selectively soliciting viewpoints supportive of mine.

- ☐ Using directive questions to control the conversation.

- ☐ Speaking as the authority and bringing in my credentials, knowledge base and contacts.

- ☐ Making condescending comments like "Everyone knows . . ." or "Any intelligent person would . . ."

- ☐ Personally attacking those who persist in opposing me.

- ☐ Blaming others.

When threatened, I typically *Flee* by:
- ☐ Sharing only limited pieces of information.

- ☐ Making agreements to get critics off my back and/or please them.

- ☐ Endorsing ideas presented at formal meetings, and then attacking their merit later in hallways and parking lots.

- ☐ Using jokes, sarcasm, or snide remarks to convey how I really feel.

- ☐ Glossing over problems or appeasing those with whom I fear conflict.

☐ Changing the subject or disguising my feelings.

☐ Harboring concerns that go unannounced and yet expect resolution.

☐ Pretending not to be hurt when I am.

☐ Hiding my motives and beliefs behind questions.

☐ Quietly moving away from uncomfortable conversations.

☐ Avoiding those with whom I differ; skirting issues.

☐ "Numbing-out" with Internet surfing, drinking, eating, smoking, shopping, sex, TV, etc.

The behaviors you checked above comprise the outward form of the defensive routine you are using in this situation. Extend some compassionate curiosity and ask yourself which one of the four common fears you are experiencing:

In this situation, I'm afraid of being seen as:
(pick one)

☐ Stupid / Foolish / Idiotic

☐ A Pretender / A Fraud

☐ An Outcast / Rejected / Unlovable

☐ Powerless / Weak / Ineffective

Notice how your fear drives you into self-protective *Fight* and *Flight* behaviors. If you listen carefully, you might even hear the short story you use to justify your behavior. It will be a version of "why I am right and the other is wrong." Armed with this self-knowledge, you are ready to...

2. Have a Breakthrough Conversation

ARE YOU WILLING TO OFFER your leadership to turn your breakdown into a breakthrough? What intentions for a better relationship or improved performance do you have? Cognitive psychologists point out that people don't do things without a reason. So now get interested in the other person's point of view. Initiate a conversation with that person. Use open-ended questions to invite him/her to tell their story about the upset. For example, you might ask:

- What are your feelings about x?

- What matters most to you about that?

- Why have you approached x the way you have?

- What are your ideas about x?

- What would you really like?

- What more can you say about that so I can understand?

- I do not want to continue until I understand what you see and feel that I don't. Please tell me more about how you see it.

- What am I doing that upsets or concerns you?

Genuine, curious inquiring enables you to have *breakthrough conversations*. In a *breakthrough conversation*, you don't assume that you know the other person's intent, and you have an appreciation for the way they process information that is different than yours. To shift into a *breakthrough conversation*, you must leave behind the filters of right/wrong and agree/disagree.

From this position, you can't hold the view that you "already know," because you are listening for something new. You might be amazed at what you didn't know about this person and his or her perceptions.

If you don't have the luxury of having a conversation with the person on the other side of your upset, you could practice putting yourself in the place of those who are chapping your hide. Reflect upon this question: "What must he/she be thinking such that his/her actions make sense to him or her?" At some level everyone's behavior makes "sense" to them. We all always have an internally valid "story" that justifies our actions. The leader's challenge is to set aside his/her "story" long enough to imagine or hear other peoples'. Inside these stories you'll often see others' fears; then you might help them move beyond their fears and step into their higher intentions. The two of you can now create agreements around new and different actions that will help you achieve the results that the two of you want.

The ability to capitalize on defensive routines in order to bring about the results leaders are committed to is a skill every leader needs. Without it leaders will be at the mercy of their defensive routines, which usually compromise, and sometimes doom, performance.

It probably goes without saying that *using* your defensive routines, as opposed to being ambushed by them, is a refinement of fear management. You'll begin being in control by learning to notice when one of your fears has been triggered. This in itself takes intention and discipline.

3. *Scout for Organizational Defensive Routines*

DEFENSIVE ROUTINES ARE UBIQUITOUS and inescapable in every organization. They are nothing more than the matrix of individual self-preservation behavior present in all groups.

"Defensive routines exist," writes Harvard professor Chris Argyris. "They are undiscussable. They proliferate and grow underground. And the social pollution is hard to identify until something occurs that blows things open."

One way to scout for defensive routines is to examine breakdowns or knotty problems and draw people out about what isn't being discussed. (Obviously, Wall Street and government leaders could have done it with the volatile risks of derivatives. The organizational defensive routine operating in Congress was classic Flight, with deference to Greenspan as "the smartest guy in the room with whom we do not disagree.")

People sometimes stop themselves from speaking their "truth" in organizational settings. Is that happening in your team? What are the "lines" your people will not cross? Ask them. Examples my partners and I have seen in the executive meeting room include:

- You never tell the emperor that he isn't wearing any clothes: no corrective feedback to the boss.

- Since the loudest person wins the argument, be loud.

- Information is power. Don't share it.

- When in doubt or in trouble, blame someone else.

- Go along to get along. Don't be the dissenting voice.

If you find reluctance among people to talk openly, you need to find a way to allow them to speak privately, anonymously. It goes without saying that people must never be reprimanded or punished for speaking truthfully about matters that threaten the company's health.

Once the gremlins lurking in organizational defensive routines have been identified, address them with your team openly, utilizing requests, offers and promises. Request suggestions about how to banish the gremlins. You can offer your own ideas. Then commit to acting on the best ideas. Enroll everyone on your team in monitoring your team's behaviors. Practice catching yourselves as the old routines get triggered during the stressful moments in your meetings and other conversations. Ask for and practice healthy alternative actions.

If your team is able, you may also want to shine the light of day upon the fears behind your team's defensive routines. Talk about what each of you can do to help mitigate these fears. Make some new promises to each other.

4. Move Beyond Your Bad Moods, Quickly

AT ANY GIVEN TIME, beyond the obvious operational problems, missed metrics and interpersonal breakdowns, there are likely one or two things that aren't immediately discernable, but yet leave you in a bad mood. Keep a constant watch for those areas. They may manifest as irritability, sourness, grumpiness, mild depression or even sleepiness. Not only do they represent opportunities for organizational improvement, they are opportunities for personal development.

All too often I've seen executives needlessly burdened by an unexamined bad mood. Once you identify the dissatisfier, create a pathway for action out of the negative story toward a positive story, one that is more likely to get you where you want to go. This second phase is critical. Large, general negative assessments, whether about circumstances or individuals, are counterproductive. Whenever you find that you have them, begin by asking where you have stopped yourself as a leader by blaming others or the circumstance itself for your dissatisfaction. Clearly, in the never-ending pursuit of absolute personal accountability, this is a moment of truth. The real question is what can *you* do to correct the situation? Armed with some ideas, create an action path that might lead to your satisfaction and the organization's betterment.

If you are unable to reach such an insight on your own, this is a perfect opportunity to work with an executive coach or some other objective observer. All of us need the help of others from time to time to see what we can't see by ourselves. Most of the time, reaching out for such assistance will help you clarify an action path.

This doesn't always work, however. Sometimes we just can't shake the hold a negative story has on us. When that happens, and you simply can't identify an action path toward possibility, try to lay down your negative story. If you don't, the story will have you, and your leadership performance will be compromised in direct proportion to the strength of your dissatisfaction's hold on you.

"I can't get no satisfaction" is the worst refrain any leader can have. In this sense, personal satisfaction is Job No. 1 for all leaders.

Dissatisfaction is obviously one signal of a breakdown. Like all other breakdowns, you can turn it into a breakthrough. Make no mistake: simply letting go of a dissatisfaction you can't correct is a powerful breakthrough itself.

CHAPTER SEVEN

CREATE THE TRUTH
Snakes, Mirages and the "Real" World

"The mind creates 'reality' and then says, 'I didn't do it.'"
—DAVID BOHM

AMONG THE WRECKAGE caused by the crash of Wall
Street's Monster through the china shop of global finance
lay a piece of debris so telling as to all but prove what really
caused the crash. *New Yorker* magazine writer John Cassidy
found it and put it on display in his March 31, 2008 profile of
former Merrill Lynch CEO E. Stanley O'Neal.

"Talking over coffee with a visitor to his apartment not
long ago, O'Neal compared running a major Wall Street
firm to being an astronaut on the doomed Challenger space
shuttle," wrote Cassidy. "He described how the engineers
check everything and say that it's all systems go. Then an
O-ring that hasn't been tested at the right temperature fails,
and disaster results. When he was at Merrill, O'Neal said, he
used to invoke the Challenger frequently. He added that he
had never imagined that he himself would figure in such a
calamity."

O'Neal, in other words, had a bumper sticker view of
the Challenger explosion: stuff happens. That conclusion, in

view of the evidence uncovered from the exhaustive investigation of the shuttle tragedy, bore a troubling similarity to the learned helplessness that led Ford customers to buy the Expedition. It also exemplified the passivity (read: failure) on the part of O'Neal and other leaders that contributed to the Bust of '08.

Stuff, as in acts of God, does indeed happen. But aeronautical and financial disasters aren't that kind of stuff. It is the job of leaders to know the difference.

Not only did this distinction appear to escape O'Neal, he seemed unaware of the striking similarities between the crashes of the Challenger and Merrill Lynch. In both cases fear-contaminated decision-making played a central role. That makes unconscious leadership a prime suspect in both catastrophes.

In both cases fear-contaminated decision-making played a central role. That makes unconscious leadership a prime suspect in both catastrophes.

On the morning of Jan. 28, 1986, seventy-three seconds after blast-off, the space shuttle Challenger exploded across America's TV screens in a silent puff of smoke. Its crew of seven was killed. As when the Twin Towers collapsed fifteen years later, the media seared the tragedy's image into the global psyche, in all likelihood sculpting human synapses for generations to come.

Three weeks after the Challenger exploded, National Public Radio News aired a story that exposed troubling underpinnings of the event. Engineers at Morton Thiokol, makers of the infamous O-rings, told NPR reporters they actually expected the O-rings to fail earlier than they did. Amazingly, those particular engineers didn't even expect Challenger to clear the launch tower before a fireball engulfed it.

So why hadn't the engineers spoken out? They were afraid, they told NPR, of losing their jobs. They were so afraid, in fact, that they would not allow their names to be used nor their voices to be recorded.

As Cassidy wrote in his *New Yorker* profile, O'Neal, too, presided over a culture that scared people into silence. "One former Merrill executive told me that the firm's top managers were too intimidated by O'Neal to bring him bad news. 'There was no one who could stand up to Stan and tell him what was really happening,' the former executive said."

And, just as at NASA, bad news hung over Wall Street and Merrill Lynch like low clouds. As the real estate/credit crisis of Wall Street's Monster approached, the Merrill Lynch board of directors either didn't see it, or pretended not to. The board made a decision that, as Cassidy reported, exacerbated the firm's risk. It approved an incentive package for Merrill's senior executives to hit benchmarks for improving return on equity.

Merrill's executives did the board's bidding by reducing the firm's capital (equity). That not only made the increased yields that Merrill subsequently posted illusory, it precariously extended the company's debt leverage at the worst possible time. The incentive triggered by the illusion of increased profitability bumped C.E.O. E. Stanley O'Neal's annual salary spectacularly, from $30 million in 2005 to $48 million in 2006.

Then, the subprime mortgage market collapsed in the summer of 2007. In hindsight, O'Neal's stunning raise could easily be seen as an $18 million attaboy for leading a bastion of global finance off a cliff. Here was a portrait of leadership so deeply unconscious as to suggest a kind of sleepwalking. Things at NASA weren't much different.

Less than six months after the Challenger explosion, William R. Lucas, director of NASA's Marshall Space Flight Center, was forced to resign because of his role in the disaster. Dr. Lucas was literally one of the world's first rocket scientists. But evidence suggests that Lucas had been a victim of his own faulty reasoning. For some nine years Lucas had been aware that the O-rings would fail at low temperatures. It was an urgent safety issue.

Here was a portrait of leadership so deeply unconscious as to suggest a kind of sleepwalking.

The nation could only expect that Lucas's resignation signaled NASA had embarked on a new learning curve. Such mismanagement would surely never again be tolerated.

Yet, in 2003, seventeen years later, the Columbia space shuttle similarly exploded, also killing its entire crew.

Autopsies of both calamities pointed to an unchanged corporate culture.

The Presidential commission appointed to investigate the Challenger disaster, headed by former Secretary of State William P. Rogers, featured some of the most illustrious names in aviation. The two hundred twenty-five-page Rogers Commission Report found that NASA's own organizational culture doomed its astronauts and their spaceship.

The press piled on. In its June 9, 1986 issue, *Time* magazine wrote that while it took NASA only a few days to determine the mechanical reason for Challenger's explosion—the defective O-rings—"the root cause of the tragedy ran deeper. A presidential commission discovered NASA itself was deeply flawed... In retrospect, it began to seem, the Challenger tragedy was all but inevitable."

In 2003, like the Rogers Commission before it, the Columbia Accident Investigation Board also issued a lengthy finding, a two-hundred-forty-eight-page report. It, too, laid much of the blame on NASA's own organizational culture.

"Ineffective leadership" was the scathing verdict.

As with Challenger, the experts discovered, the cause of the explosion was a structural problem long known to management—in this case defective foam insulating panels—that defeated Columbia and her crew. Said the investigators: "The board strongly believes that if these persistent, systemic flaws are not resolved, the scene is set for another accident."

NASA promised to overhaul itself, but it seemed stuck in its own Groundhog Day of endlessly repeated errors. Under the headline "Why NASA Can't Get It Right," *Time* magazine reported in its August 1, 2005, issue: "Despite assurances that it was safe to launch [the shuttle] Discovery, several pieces of foam broke free during takeoff last week, forcing an embarrassed NASA to put all future flights on hold..."

Maybe it was time to end the space shuttle program, opined *Time*.

If Mr. O'Neal's subordinates and the Morton Thiokol engineers had been courageous enough to speak out, their courage alone wouldn't have been a panacea for Wall Street or NASA. But they would have set in motion very different forces, those of consciousness.

Such public chastisement seemed to have little impact inside NASA. When NPR did a follow-up report on the twentieth anniversary of the Challenger tragedy, in 2006, the same engineers who had told NPR twenty years earlier that they expected the O-rings to fail still insisted on anonymity. The role of fear in NASA's corporate culture had apparently not changed.

This was the telling debris shard *New Yorker* writer Cassidy uncovered when he profiled the former head of Merrill Lynch: that NASA's rocket scientists, and that E. Stanley O'Neal, a man of inspiring achievement—he was the first African-American head of a major Wall Street bank— would see themselves as helpless victims of a situation that they played an active role in creating. This is compelling evidence of unconsciousness.

The point here is not to second-guess anyone—not Mr. O'Neal, Morton Thiokol, NASA, Wall Street, not anyone. As Dr. Taleb points out in *The Black Swan*, Monday morning quarterbacking, even though its purpose may be to improve future decision-making, is mostly a waste of time. This is because of "the fundamental, severe, and incurable unpredictability of the world." In other words, what might have resulted from other decisions is forever unknowable. What is certain, however, is that alternative decisions would also have yielded unpredictable results, some of which might also have proved undesirable.

If Mr. O'Neal's subordinates and the Morton Thiokol engineers had been courageous enough to speak out, their courage alone wouldn't have been a panacea for Wall Street or NASA. But they would have set in motion very different forces, those of consciousness.

Our concern is not decisions, per se, but the mix of consciousness and unconsciousness that generates them. The cyclical nature of near-disaster followed by taxpayer bailout that has plagued the American economy lo these many decades clearly shows that the mix needs changing. Because leaders get paid to produce results, nothing can be more fundamental to every leader's task than learning how to cultivate and sustain an optimum mixture of consciousness.

Because of the structure of the brain and the organism it serves, complete consciousness is neither possible nor desirable. What is both possible and mandated by the power of our technological prowess is a consciousness mixture rich enough to let us create the truth from our quicksilver circumstances.

By "creating the truth" I'm not talking about doing something nefarious, like obscuring or distorting facts. Quite the opposite. I'm talking about exposing facts to as much awareness and interpretation as possible.

Creating the truth is about going beyond the mere truth of things as they now seem to the "generative" truth of possibilities beyond the limits of our current perceptions and beliefs. This requires overcoming the fear of others' points of view. I use the term generative, because the behavioral processes described here involve continuous shared exploration and discovery. They *generate* truth that can be found no other way.

> Creating the truth is about going beyond the mere truth of things as they now seem to the "generative" truth of possibilities beyond the limits of our current perceptions and beliefs.

In the face of obstacles, creating generative truth takes us through and around and over them to our goals. Generative truth is a kind of jailbreak. It liberates us from the synaptic prison of our own stories.

Generative truth is created through three interlocking relationships.

The first relationship is between one's reflective self— what we're calling the conscious self—and the reflexive self, the unconscious self.

The second is between the reflective self and the reflexive (default) selves of others. The conscious leader's task is to create more self-reflection among colleagues.

This leads to the third relationship, which takes place among reflective selves. The possibility of that relationship is the whole reason for this book.

Each of us begins to create the truth by starting to observe our reflexive, or knee-jerk, selves. Because of the awesome power of the unconscious brain, this is easier said than done. The default self is a vital life partner; its job is keeping us safe. Our mission here is learning to recognize just how often we respond reflexively and to note when greater consciousness, reflection, would serve better.

The more self-reflective you are, the more dynamic, generative and creative are your relations with others. New horizons of possibilities open up.

The more ideological you are, or the less often you think of the common good, the more chronically frightened you are, or the more unresolved trauma you have in your life, the harder it is to kick the habit of counterproductive reflexive behavior. For some individuals (we've all known a few), giving up cigarettes or crack cocaine may be easier than becoming self-reflective.

The good news is that once the process of self-reflection begins, one's relationships with other people automatically change. The more self-reflective you are, the more dynamic, generative and creative are your relations with others. New horizons of possibilities open up.

And when leaders develop the ability to inspire self-reflection on the part of others, and to nurture relationships among the self-reflective, they midwife the birth of new worlds.

If you think about it, you will realize this is hardly a radical or controversial idea. It is, after all, where the notion of democracy came from. Its basis, as James Surowiecki writes in his superb book, *The Wisdom of Crowds*, is the "powerful truth" that "under the right circumstances, groups are remarkably intelligent, and are often smarter than the smartest people among them."

To understand the difference between mere truth and generative truth consider the situation of our friend J.D.

J.D. presented his board with a compelling and distressing set of facts. His conclusion: a viral liquidity crisis loomed over the global economy. There was no place to hide. The organism of international finance needed to heal the infection, and leadership from companies like his was critical.

The mere truth was also that J.D. was angry and

> Creating the truth requires us to accept that the "story" produced by this habit of mind is not the "truth." Rather, it is our own unique internal representation of the world around us.

disappointed with his board's response so far. He was suspicious of the motivations of his friend in hiring him. And he was also more than a little concerned that his own reputation could be sullied.

From these mere truths, J.D. would like to lead his company into action that is congruent with values and goals capable of helping the company meet its challenges.

Creating the truth, as set forth here, is a process that would help J.D. do that.

Creating the truth begins with the humble recognition that we have an inescapable reflexive behavioral repertoire—a habit of mind that colors our every perception.

Next, creating the truth requires us to accept that the "story" produced by this habit of mind is not the "truth." Rather, it is our own unique internal representation of the world around us. The world around us is always "out there," an endlessly changing motion picture, never the same from one moment to the next. Our internal depiction of this state of affairs is forever destined to be more like a snapshot, or a series of freeze frames, than a mirror of life's ceaseless flow.

Good thing, too. Otherwise, we couldn't function.

This is not to say we're delusional in the sense that we walk down the street talking to an invisible six-foot-tall rabbit. It is to say, however, that we want to become as expert as possible in grasping the role of consciousness in the creation of reality.

So the question for leaders is how to assemble the interpretations of circumstances—and strategies for addressing them—most likely to help them achieve their goals.

Creating the truth, then, consists of a tandem examination of intentions and beliefs.

Clarifying intentions, as we saw in the preceding chapter, results from the most intimate kind of soliloquy. We privately pose a critical question to what we call our "self." Namely, what do we intend? There are no eavesdroppers, no judges. There's nobody here but us. Because the intentions that emerge from this self-inquiry are the most purely truthful that we can imagine, they have the greatest latent power to energize us and unleash our maximum creativity.

For their part, beliefs are the reinforcing beams of our intentions. But they have inherent weakness.

For their part, beliefs are the reinforcing beams of our intentions. But they have inherent weakness. In evaluating the usefulness of our beliefs to serve our intentions, it is essential to remember their mirage-like, fictitious character. It is handiest to think of beliefs as stories, built-up stories. Running accounts of the past.

Our own story is just one of the countless abstractions continuously being made all around us by others. Because of this, humanity's stories can't help being a hazy mirage created by the nature of the psyche, and the atmospheric conditions of nearly seven billion psyches, in the same way mountains and oceans create weather.

"A civilization which cannot burst through its current abstractions is doomed to sterility after a very limited period of progress," Alfred North Whitehead wrote in *Science and the Modern World*.

Still, beliefs are real enough to commit us to action and its consequences. But they are not so real as to be immutable. We can change our beliefs.

Sometimes we change beliefs almost automatically—as when events show us their error. More often, however, our beliefs prove too hard for us to shake. That clearly was the case when NASA couldn't straighten up and fly right even after the Challenger disaster exposed its deadly organizational culture. Similarly, the ominous implications of the failure of Long-Term Capital Management—proof that the dangerous investment products known as derivatives threatened global economic stability—were lost on Greenspan and other leaders. As a direct result, the world economy suffered a historic blow.

Changing beliefs actually does involve growing new body parts in the brain. This is the "reality" of belief that is critical for leaders to understand.

What these cases show about our stubborn resistance to facts is that changing our beliefs, or the beliefs of others, can feel as difficult as growing a new body part. That's because changing beliefs actually does involve growing new body parts in the brain. This is the "reality" of belief that is critical for leaders to understand.

Most of us think of ourselves as pretty good at judging facts. Few of us, however, are very good at calibrating the instrument—the synaptic mind—with which we judge those facts. The classic Indian fable of the blindfolded men describing the elephant illustrates this point. No amount of words will let the man feeling the "rope" of the tail convince the man groping the "pillar" of the leg that the pillar is a rope. Only an idiot would confuse a rope with a pillar.

We evaluate facts, then, against the template of our

beliefs. Thus do we tend to see what we believe, as much of the world's turmoil attests.

The tragedy of the Challenger and the rampage of Wall Street's Monster are less sagas of misguided policies and pedestrian errors than textbook examples of unconscious leadership.

They also point to great opportunities for executive coaching. Had my team and I been emplaced by President Bill Clinton, I would have—to begin with—been very clear about why the evidence suggested that a moment of urgent need for conscious leadership was at hand.

In the privacy of my coaching relationship with the various parties, I would have had very explicit discussions about the evidence, as I see it, that all concerned—the President, the Treasury secretary, the Federal Reserve Board, the SEC, and the U.S. Congress itself—were failing to lead.

> Interpretations of important subjects that differ as widely as did those of Greenspan and Commodity Futures Trading Commission Chairwoman Brooksley Born on the danger of derivatives always signal the need for conscious leadership.

Interpretations of important subjects that differ as widely as did those of Greenspan and Commodities Futures Trading Commission Chairwoman Brooksley Born on the danger of derivatives *always* signal the need for conscious leadership. Conscious leadership requires not merely a contest of ideas, but deep engagement between divergent beliefs.

It is that engagement, and only that engagement, that has the potential to create new and better truth.

Considering data or ideas that conflict with one's beliefs is one of the most difficult behaviors in the human repertoire; it leads us directly to one another's synaptic barriers—a line in the neurons. What typically takes place in this setting is confrontation ranging from argument to war. These are not circumstances in which the truth—meaning *new* perspectives, possibilities and solutions—can be created. Confrontation is not engagement, as I use the term. It is a synaptically driven rejection of engagement.

What is needed is to get behind the eyes of others, and into their hearts. As defined here, the truth can only be created from a platform of mutually understood beliefs. While human beings are genetically wired to achieve such empathy, attaining it is often difficult, thanks, no doubt, to the powerful fight-or-flight survival mechanism and the evolutionary history that produced it.

Because deep engagement among differing beliefs is so difficult, it requires explicit leadership practices to dependably access it.

Because deep engagement among differing beliefs is so difficult, it requires explicit leadership practices to dependably access it.

The following five practices are proven truth creators.

PRACTICES

1. Keep a "Snake List"

A GOOD DRILL for limbering up your truth-creation skill is to keep a list of current problems, including relationship breakdowns. I call this a snake list. Make a habit of selecting one of these problems (one of these "snakes") for study.

See how many missed signs that led up to the problem you can discover. Because of the clarity of hindsight, after the fact they usually stand out like neon markers.

Talk to others who are also aware of, or wrestling with, the problem. In particular, seek out those who may have attempted to call attention to the problem before it materialized. Get their views on missed signs and opportunities.

Note: this is not a practice in assigning blame or indulging in regrets. It's the beginning of a continuous improvement workout intended to heighten your powers of observation. Simply keeping a small list of problems is deceptively powerful, because we tend to bury them. High achievement people are especially prone to this.

Keeping a snake list is the first step in becoming a good snake handler. It involves awareness of the problem first, which is consciousness, and then having a relationship with the problem other than denial or resistance. Obviously, problems can't be solved by denying their existence. Neither are they solved by fighting them, because what we resist persists. Problems, like snakes, are best handled by awareness, understanding, and good technique.

2. Be Interested vs. Interesting

AT LEAST ONCE A DAY engage someone in a conversation in which you are far more interested in what they say than in what you say to them. Look for statements that cause you real curiosity and—within the bounds of good taste—indulge your curiosity. Don't be nosey, just genuinely interested.

Among the things to be interested in: items from your snake list above. How do others see those snakes?

As your skills develop, look for opportunities to repeat this practice as many times daily as possible. When you're ready, try it at parties; notice what happens.

Deep, sincere interest in the ideas, concerns, thoughts, perspectives, and lives of others is your goal.

3. Turn Complaints into Requests

NOURISH AN INABILITY TO IGNORE GRIPES. If colleagues, subordinates or customers lodge a complaint, learn to take notice. Treat every complaint as an invitation to take creative action to transform it.

The first creative action is to turn complaints into requests. "This room is too hot, dammit!" becomes,

"Could you please turn the thermostat down?" "I hate the way our CEO runs meetings!" becomes "Would you please start meetings on time and get immediately to the business at hand and leave socializing for lunch?" The request is generative. The complaint is not. This also exposes invalid complaints, because the request looks silly.

Start by taking seriously your own complaints. (Such as, "The board ignored my request.")

Write down the complaint, and then list the actions you plan to take to eliminate the complaint. Establish deadlines. Stay in action by keeping a journal of your thoughts and efforts until the complaint is removed. Be sure to make a journal entry about when the complaint was overcome and how you did it.

When you get good at this for yourself, as subtly as possible try to assist others in doing the same thing. Don't be boorish or pedantic. Don't give advice. Using your skills of curiosity, try to solicit the complainant's own ideas for resolving the situation. Try to be so stealthy in your efforts that people just feel the balm of your sincere interest.

4. Depose Ideology

IDEOLOGIES OFTEN ARE resistant to evidence to the contrary. An ideologue is a true believer who does not want to consider new data and the emerging understanding it can bring.

Wall Street's Monster exposed Greenspan as such an idealogue.

"A professed libertarian, he counted among his formative influences the novelist Ayn Rand, who portrayed collective power as an evil force set against the enlightened self-interest of individuals," reported *The New York Times.* "In turn, he showed a resolute faith that those participating in financial markets would act responsibly."

In the wake of the destruction caused by Wall Street's Monster, Greenspan was forced to confess his "shocked disbelief" about how wrong he had been.

We propose that positions rooted in ideology be replaced by informed "stands." A stand is a rational, ethical commitment to a course of action based on facts, as they are understood. Stands are inherently flexible. They change as factual understanding changes.

They change, in other words, as you find new, more useful assessments of those facts.

This is a challenging practice that may well require outside assistance. Because of the subjective nature of perception, we might not always know when we are succumbing to fact-resistant ideology. Because of the hazard of that condition, we might have a hard time 'fessing up to it, even if we sense its presence in our thinking.

Convert your positions to stands by asking those closest to you to assess your handling of the most important challenges of the moment. Specifically, do they have a view of the facts that differs sharply from yours? If so, how do they rate your openness to the facts as they see them?

If they rank you poorly, consider seeking advice on whether your views need adjusting. If you conclude that they do, begin seeking ways to take a stand based on your new understanding.

The more resistant you find yourself to this practice, the more you need it. If you find that you just can't shake yourself free of your habitual position or ideology, consider the radical surgery of the next practice.

5. Constructive Dialogue

THIS IS A VARIATION on a dialectic tool that has been around since at least the time of Socrates. Every lawyer is familiar with its basic tenets. It's about learning to argue a case from opposing points of view. For high-judgment decisions, those with high stakes, this is an essential tool.

We need cooperative controversy, because we live in an inherently uncertain world. That uncertainty creates controversy. We can't escape controversy, so we need to embrace it as the potential ally that it is. We do that by *cooperating* in its exploration. That's the purpose of this practice.

Constructive dialogue puts ideas on trial, not people. It does this through role-playing. Those playing the protagonist's role suggest actions, solutions, advocate plans. Antagonists critique and challenge, offer constructive feedback, point out logical flaws and missing ideas, examine probable effects of particular actions, explore the likely emotional reactions of stakeholders.

Take a pending corporate decision and have the most persuasive protagonist and antagonist argue it as forcefully as they can from their perspectives.

Then have them switch roles. Because they have just experienced their counterparts playing these roles with sincerity and passion, they now have a powerful aid in embracing the other perspective. In constructive dialogue, integrity is everything. To get the most out of it you have to play the roles from your heart. You have to mean it.

Every lawyer knows the power of this practice for developing a nimble mind and a degree of understanding of others.

Here's the difference in the way I teach constructive dialogue for the purpose of nurturing conscious leadership. I want the discussion to go beneath ideas to the subterranean region of feelings and needs. This, of course, is where common humanity is found. It's also the only vantage point from which generative truth can be created.

Had I been coaching Greenspan and Born, I would have guided them through this practice. If they did it earnestly, witnesses (Congress and President Clinton, for instance) would have known if they had achieved the ability to understand and express not only what each other was thinking, but what they were feeling, what they were scared of. If they hadn't achieved that level of empathy, observers would have known that, too.

Empathy, of course, is the key. Humanity has a genius for it, this ability to embrace interests beyond our own basic needs. We regularly stir ourselves with its demonstration. But how irregularly we achieve it can be seen in the size of our militaries and the destructive power of our weapons.

If we hope to create generative truth through conscious leadership, achieving true empathy is grindingly pragmatic. It goes far beyond "ethics" and "morality" to frontiers of possibility we have only begun to glimpse.

CHAPTER EIGHT

THE DISCREET CHARM
OF THE HONEST MESS

**The key to Quicksilver performance:
don't believe everything you think**

*"You have to do something **right** to get an error."*
—BILL JAMES

BASEBALL, the great American pastime, has an embedded illusion that turns out to be a great American metaphor.
For more than a century, as the sport evolved from its rustic
origins into a colorful pageant, contests were won and lost
based on subtleties that were invisible to even the most experienced observers. You couldn't watch a baseball game and
believe your eyes to understand what you had seen. Neither
could you consult the sport's conventional statistics and
make much more sense of the field of play. There was a hidden drama going on. It took an elegant essayist and prickly
contrarian named Bill James to point it out.

James brought a new interpretation to baseball's statistics
to show that the game's conventional way of counting and
interpreting pivotal events—errors, walks, and runs batted
in, for instance—actually created a field of illusion. That made
effective management of both teams and players impossible.

Errors, noted James, involved a dubious moral judgment.
He wrote that the error "is, without exception, the only major

statistic in sports which is a record of what an observer thinks *should have been accomplished.*"

Thus, errors lived in the record books as mistakes. That, however, was a misleading impression. A fielder savvy enough to play a hitter correctly, or fast enough to get his glove on a hard-hit ball, was actually exhibiting skill—as James saw it, "you have to do something *right* to get an error." That skill could be much more valuable to a team than its absence in a slower, less knowledgeable player who was making fewer errors.

Similar misconceptions applied to the sport's canon on walks and RBIs. A walk was neutral on a player's resume—it neither hurt nor harmed his batting average, yet a batter with an eye, and psyche (it takes both), keen enough to earn bases on balls exerted a lot of pressure on the opposition. As for RBIs, they simply gave more credit to hitters than they were due—runners had to first be on base in order for them to be batted in.

"The problem is that baseball statistics are not pure accomplishments of men against other men, which is what we are in the habit of seeing them as," James wrote. "They are accomplishments of men in combination with their circumstances."

James was a born iconoclast. He had a "preference for leaving an honest mess for others to clean up rather than a tidy lie for them to admire," writes the acclaimed financial author Michael Lewis in his book, *Moneyball*.

Billy Beane, general manager of the Oakland A's, used James's insights so spectacularly to clean up the particular mess on his hands that Lewis wrote *Moneyball* about it.

Beane's mess was that the new owner of his team had imposed a harsh cap on player salaries.

At the time Beane became the A's general manager, 1998, veteran scouts rated draft prospects based on such bizarre criteria as "Good Body" and "Good Face," as well as on misleading statistics.

Beane used James's statistical insights and a brainy assistant with a laptop computer—the assistant happened to be a distinguished Harvard economics graduate—to detect player talents that were quite literally invisible to others. Those talents showed up in player statistics *if* you knew how to read the statistics. This was the equivalent of a sharp-eyed investor finding hidden value that was being overlooked by the market.

As Lewis wrote, "there was a bias toward what people saw with their own eyes, or thought they had seen. The human mind played tricks on itself when it relied exclusively on what it saw, and every trick it played was a financial opportunity for someone who saw through the illusion to the reality. There was a lot you couldn't see when you watched a baseball game."

"At the opening of the 2002 season, the richest team, the New York Yankees, had a payroll of $126 million, while the two poorest teams, the Oakland A's and the Tampa Bay Devil Rays, had payrolls of less that a third of that, about $40 million," Lewis wrote in his 2003 book.

With his newfound statistics, Billy Beane and the Oakland A's sparked a revolution.

"For the past several years," wrote Lewis, "working with either the lowest or next to lowest payroll in the game, the

Oakland A's had won more regular season games than any other team, except the Atlanta Braves."

Moreover, the A's "had paid about half a million dollars per win," contrasted with teams like the Baltimore Orioles or Texas Rangers, whose victories carried an individual price tag of close to $3 million. That meant the A's were getting a return on investment six hundred percent greater than their richer competitors.

And that's why baseball is such a great metaphor, not just for the American condition but for the human condition. The Oakland A's made hay from the honest mess of their relatively small pocketbook. Turns out that while money is important in winning baseball games, as in life, money isn't everything. What Billy Beane did was take the fat pitch of a paradox and drive it into the nosebleed section.

That's what you can do with a paradox—*if* you can keep from being scared stupid by it. But that's a big "if."

The moment you stop believing everything you think is when your thinking really begins...

Life can't help being something of a mess, says the famous protagonist in *Charlotte's Web*, E.B. White's classic children's story. Charlotte, of course, is a spider. The mess she's referring to is the necessity of trapping and eating flies.

Charlotte's fans don't have to deal with the mess of dining on flies. They do, however, have to contend with the mess of paradoxes. And there are a lot more paradoxes in the world than flies. Paradoxes, in fact, are everywhere. You can't get away from them. Quicksilver performance is impossible unless you can handle them.

That's why it's critical to recognize paradoxes for the gift they really are. Hidden in every paradox is the potential for a new way of seeing the world. That's why you must learn to view paradoxes properly, which is to say honestly. It's also why you have to learn not to trust what you think you're seeing in a paradox.

The moment you stop believing everything you think is when your thinking really begins.

Just because a problem looks insoluble doesn't mean that it is. Just because a guy doesn't *look* like a great baseball player doesn't mean that he can't win games for you and make you a hero with the team's accountants.

A paradox, just to review, is two simultaneously existing conditions that appear to be mutually exclusive. Like being a truth-teller and a company team player; a great CEO and a great parent; having an autonomous local hospital that is perfectly responsive to community needs and yet part of a large, efficient health care system. The list is infinite.

Car companies selling cars that are temporarily profitable but so ultimately out of synch with market trends that they will cause the companies' collapse are dealing with paradox. Same with food vendors whose products are engineered to over-stimulate the appetite, causing obesity, undermining health. Ditto "investment" firms peddling products with hidden liabilities that end up destroying wealth. Ditto every company whose manufacturing processes damage the environment upon which life on earth depends. The same is true of every individual earning a "living" in ways that sap joy and hasten dying.

The messiest part of paradoxes isn't their apparent

contradictions, it's that they scare the bejeezus out of us. They typically scare us into denial. In fact, "scare" may put it too mildly. Our true response to some paradoxes is probably more like terror.

Imagine messages in Detroit's SUV ads admitting what Keith Bradsher reported about the products in his book, *High and Mighty—SUVs: The World's Most Dangerous Vehicles and How They Got that Way.* Imagine food chains advertising that some of their fare is carefully engineered to contain levels of sugar, fat and salt, as former US Food and Drug Administration commissioner David A. Kessler, MD, writes in his book, *The End of Overeating—Taking Control of the Insatiable American Diet,* that make them nearly as addictive as cocaine. Or what if Wall Street had publicly acknowledged that the derivatives it was selling to investors really were "weapons of financial mass destruction," as Warren Buffett warned?

Such "candor deficits" aren't just a kind of delusional behavior. For leadership purposes they actually represent willful unconsciousness of the most potentially dangerous kind. It's a little like preferring life-or-death sprints to the emergency room over routine check-ups. I believe that our current economic crisis, and perhaps the majority of humanity's most important challenges today, can be seen as failures of paradox management, private and collective.

This quirk of human nature is captured by a May 25, 2009, *New Yorker* cartoon in which two passersby encounter a telling scene: Wall Street's iconic charging bull statue is being changed out for an ostrich with its head in the sand.

"I think the head's in the wrong place," allows one of the characters.

That's a funny look at one of the most serious paradoxes around. In his book about the Great Depression, *The Lords of Finance: The Bankers Who Broke the World*, Liaquat Ahamed sums up the predicament of central bankers this way:

"At times of crisis, central bankers generally believe that it is prudent to obey the admonition that mothers over the centuries have passed on to their children: 'If you can't say anything nice, don't say anything at all.' It avoids the recurring dilemma that confronts financial officials dealing with a panic—they can be honest in their public statements and thereby feed the frenzy or they can try to be reassuring, which usually entails resorting to outright untruths."

Clearly, it's a messy choice. The malevolence of Nazi Germany can be traced to economic collapse, notes Ahamed. On the other hand, the tidy lie that all is well when it isn't does nothing to address the monotony of boom and bust economic cycles, as Ahamed explains.

"By one count there have been sixty different crises since the early seventeenth century," he writes. "These bubbles and crises seem to be deep-rooted in human nature and the capitalist system… Each of these episodes differed in detail… All, however, shared a common pattern: an eerily similar cycle from greed to fear."

My training in psychology persuades me that greed is an expression of fear. And fear cannot be successfully managed with deceit. The tidy lie, then, offers no way out, which could explain the broken record-like nature of economic cycles.

Give me the honest mess of facing the *causes* of those cycles any day.

The best way I know to savor the discreet charm of the honest mess is to pose a Paradoxical Development Question to yourself. This involves choosing a particularly thorny problem in your life and then letting your subconscious *mine* it for insight. Notice I say "insight," not "solution." The Paradoxical Development Question is not about a problem to be solved. Rather, it is simply a question to be honestly lived with. When you pose a PDQ correctly, what you're saying to your subconscious is: "Don't worry your pretty little neurons about this. I'm just, well, wondering."

Fear cannot be successfully managed with deceit. The tidy lie, then, offers no way out, which could explain the broken record-like nature of economic cycles.

You pose a PDQ soothingly. You *purr* a PDQ. You *coo* a PDQ. Seduction? I hope to shout. A PDQ forces you to learn your way through a mess.

A PDQ uses your conscious mind to seduce your vastly more powerful unconscious mind. When you task the unconscious mind with sincere curiosity about how to live with some paradox that might be driving you to drink, you veritably unshackle it. Things get really—*illuminating*. The unconscious mind, supreme paradox junkie that it is, comes up with the most interesting insights. These insights—good word, what?—simply can't be found in the synaptic canyon lands of the conscious mind. They lie on the psyche's frontier, beyond the jail of habit. They can be so powerful as to hit like a miracle.

Paradox is the soul's mother country. It is to the psyche

what the briar patch is to Brer Rabbit; what a 100 mph fastball is to a great baseball hitter—all you have to do is get your bat squarely on it. The thing's own energy will turn it into a souvenir in the outfield bleachers.

How do I know? Because my clients have been telling me about it for years. I have this classic experience. I'll be weaving my way through a crowded airport, roll-aboard suitcase in tow, and some stranger with a paradox-eating grin and outstretched hand will approach.

"You don't know me, Dr. O'Brien," such encounters always begin. My greeters will then proceed to tell me they heard me present PDQ at a conference they attended and that they then applied it with powerful results. They will want to share with me their paradox and the breakthrough of their PDQ. And if I'm not rushing for a flight I *always* listen. By now, I have quite a collection of these amazing PDQ stories. The PDQ is the most powerful single tool I know of for not believing everything you think, for giving yourself a chance to think something more creative, resourceful and powerful in the face of messy challenges.

If I had my way, every leader in the world would have a Quicksilver Special Operations team in place, a "force multiplier" of creative responsiveness to our quicksilver world. And one of the first skills Quicksilver special operators would master is PDQ. There isn't a paradox in the world that could survive transformation as a result of their efforts.

Before I end with the practices below, I want to share a little scientific evidence with you of why the PDQ is so powerful.

In her provocative book, *RenGen—Renaissance Generation*, Patricia Martin points to signs that humanity is encountering the textbook conditions of renaissance. While she is basically optimistic, she is also realistic. Renaissance, she warns, confronts civilization with the prospects of both apocalypse and rebirth. And, she points out, "death comes first… It is important to understand that no matter how grim a death a society experiences, the cultural ashes that come from such a fall fertilize its soil for new growth."

It was the collapse of Rome—*umbilicus mundi*, "belly button of the world"—unimaginable at the time, and the unprecedented Black Death, that lay waste to humans and animals throughout Asia and Europe, that gave rise to the great Italian Renaissance that changed the world, notes Martin.

She quotes German scholar Willemien Otten saying that the Renaissance represented a literal "opening up" of the human mind. But what—psychologically, emotionally, neurologically—actually happened?

Martin presents dramatic evidence from a 2005 experiment in Sydney, Australia, where electroencephalographs recorded the brain activities of a hundred adults who were presented with various stimuli. When encountering familiar or expected objects or experiences, the EEGs showed, brain activity trods predictable paths. But scientists found that unexpected or unusual stimuli awakened surprising capacity.

"… they found that the entire brain gets stronger as a result of the activity; it develops 'synaptic strength' to fire faster and endure stimulation for longer periods. Finally, there is a spin-off effect in the brain that opens more ion channels for receiving information and decreases membrane resistance to more input. This is scientific evidence of what might commonly be construed as open-mindedness—an important factor in a renaissance mind-set."

So there you have it: a neurology of the open mind. This is why, when you're faced with a challenge that you don't know how to respond to, you should *never* believe what you're thinking until you've given yourself a chance to think anew. It's because the chances are very good that you aren't synaptically fit enough to manage the challenge. This could explain why some of our most important leaders mistook the financial bust of 2008 for a tsunami, and still don't understand how their own lack of synaptic fitness contributed to the crisis.

> When you're faced with a challenge that you don't know how to respond to, you should never believe what you're thinking until you've given yourself a chance to think anew.

Again, thanks to Moore's law, I believe this is the structural condition with which we must now all come to grips. To me, the evidence is simply overwhelming that a moment of renaissance—apocalypse or rebirth, maybe both—is at hand. Two aspects of this moment cry out in particular for the attention of leaders.

First, as Martin points out, the apocalyptic edge of the renaissance sword triggers the most powerful impulse in the human behavioral repertoire: the survival imperative. Any organization or individual opposing it—as are organizations vending unsafe cars, unhealthy food, and fraudulent investment products—is courting disaster. The awesome forces involved make tsunamis look like ripples. The best such organizations can hope for is to deceive as much of the market as possible for as long as possible. This is as forlorn a strategy as I know of, because it can do little more than delay the day of reckoning, if not for ourselves then for our children. Organizations and individuals seeking refuge in this strategy will ultimately reap the whirlwind, as the fates of GM, AIG, Bear Sterns, etc., suggest. It's not a question of *if*, but when.

Second, there's this business of synaptic fitness. As Dr. Kessler reports in *The End of Overeating*, functional magnetic resonance imaging (fMRI) can actually take a synaptic portrait of the brain. Kessler describes the work of Oxford University professor Edmund Rolls.

Using fMRI, "Rolls has created images of how the brain responds when it's stimulated," writes Kessler. "His work allows us to see specific neural circuits in action. For example, a neuron stimulated by a sweet taste that has been coupled with a fatty texture would be active when we eat, say, an éclair."

How do neurons stimulated by paradoxes like unsafe cars, foods and financial products respond? We can't know until we see the fMRIs. What we can easily experience, however, is the enjoyment of showing up to dance with such paradoxes instead of hiding in the shadows. And were I forced to choose only one dance move, I wouldn't hesitate to turn to the PDQ.

PRACTICES

1. Ask Yourself a "Paradoxical Development Question"

THE BOTTOM LINE is that PDQs help us face the messes of life honestly and creatively by replacing "habits that hinder." One of the most common hindering habits I know of, for instance, is not saying "no" when evidence shows "no" is the correct answer. This is essentially an unavoidable occupational hazard of organizational life, because hardly anything is more fatal to success than being perceived as not being a team player. We tend to go along with uncomfortable situations—defective O-rings, risky investment products, the poor performance/broken promises of colleagues—for just this reason. It is not a formula for successful personal or organizational life.

In such circumstances, the Paradoxical Development Question: "How can I register my objections AND be seen as a high-contributing player?" might spark panic at first. This is because the conscious mind hasn't a clue about the answer to that question. But the subconscious does, and it finds the question irresistible.

In any case, selecting PDQs to work on isn't hard. Just make a list of your biggest concerns at the moment. Next, identify the paradoxes involved—what you want and what's preventing you from getting it. Now pick one to work on.

Put a PDQ on sticky notes and place the notes where you will see them periodically throughout the day—on the bathroom mirror, the fridge, the car dashboard. I've had clients make screensavers of their PDQs. (I recommend that all leaders have a personal PDQ at all times—and only one at a time.)

Live with that PDQ for a while and see what happens. If you're typical, in no time you'll be shocked to have any number of answers pop into your head that wouldn't have occurred to you otherwise. *This* is the reason for my airport PDQ moments.

In the case of our imaginary investment bank CEO, J.D., I can guarantee that the question, "How can I serve my board AND the public interest?" would produce answers that would not otherwise be forthcoming.

An interesting PDQ for the U.S. President might be: "How can we protect the nation's interests AND generate goodwill around the world?"

That is not an easy question, but it is one, I assure you, that would give a team of assistants writers' cramps listing all the answers. The answers are clearly electrifying and life changing, because they turn adversaries into allies.

Architect William McDonough, a world leader in sustainable design, posed a powerful variation on a PDQ. He asked, "Why can't a building be like a tree?" (To convert the question to PDQ form I might propose something like: How can we create an economical building design and have it contribute to the ecosystem the way a tree does?)

McDonough conceived of what he calls the "retroactive design assignment of a tree": "Could you design something for me that purifies water, provides habitat for hundreds of species, builds soil, accrues solar income as fuel, provides food and micro-climate, makes oxygen, fixes nitrogen and sequesters carbon?"

Just asking the question helped McDonough, his partners and clients achieve results that are nothing less than transformative.

One of the other questions he asks is, "How can business be good for all the children on the planet?"

Posing such PDQs can help leaders find breakthrough solutions to all manner of "honest messes."

So what's your top PDQ? Pick up your pen and write it down.

2. Ask Yourself What You Need

As YOUR UNCONSCIOUS is mulling over your Paradoxical Development Question, take a little time for yourself.

Asking yourself what you need seems such an obvious question that it hardly merits mention. It's critical, however, for bringing habits to consciousness.

From an early age, most of us are taught not to whine. But ignoring what's bothering us does not lead to emotional literacy, either in childhood or afterward.

So, for this practice: the next time you find yourself upset or worried about something, ask yourself what need you have that is not being met.

"Unfortunately, most of us have never been taught to think in terms of needs," writes Dr. Marshall Rosenberg in his book, *Nonviolent Communication: A Language of Life*. "We are accustomed to thinking about what's wrong with other people when our needs aren't being filled." His book contains a list of forty basic human needs.

Why is that pertinent here? Many leaders subject themselves to an impossible standard of performance, as though people with their authority and income levels shouldn't have needs.

A leader in J.D.'s position, for example, could easily find himself reacting angrily without bothering to identify the specific needs underlying his anger. Those unmet needs will make it difficult, if not impossible, for him to do his job.

In Rosenberg's list, under the heading "Interdependence" are sixteen examples of human needs. They include: acceptance, appreciation, closeness, community, consideration, contribution to the enrichment of life (to exercise one's power by giving that which contributes to life), emotional safety, empathy, honesty (the empowering honesty that enables us to learn from limitations), love, reassurance, respect, support, trust, understanding, warmth.

J.D. may not need his board to love him, but to be empowered by and of service to the board, many of those needs will necessarily be met.

By learning to identify such needs, you can take responsibility for getting them met. That is a much healthier and more creative condition than enduring the cortisol soak of blaming others.

3. Ask For Forgiveness

THE WAY OF THE CONSCIOUS LEADER is the way of the student. The learner's life regularly entails the discovery that past actions were mistaken. The ability to recognize mistakes, acknowledge them, and apologize when appropriate is one of the most life-giving skills any leader can have.

Make a list of any recent mistakes that you might not have adequately acknowledged. Next, decide if you owe an apology. If you do, don't lose a minute in making it. The balm of sincere apology is not to be missed.

So encompassing is the amazing grace of seeking forgiveness, it can even be useful in situations like J.D.'s, where its applicability isn't immediately obvious.

Imagine, for instance, how J.D.'s brilliant intentionality might be served if he began his next approach to the board by apologizing for not doing more thorough research before accepting the position of CEO. What if J.D. acknowledged to his board that by not doing the research he might have inadvertently contributed to the problem? The power of such a question is obvious, because it is virtually certain that the board's contribution to the problem was inadvertent, too. The miracle of forgiveness is completion. It liberates all concerned to rejoin the community of synergistic creativity.

4. Ask Yourself the BIG Question: "What is LIFE Calling For?"

WHEN YOU FIND YOURSELF with a strong story about a breakdown, and that story is not allowing you to fix the problem or get the results you desire, that's when you want to ask the Big Question: *What is LIFE calling for?* That question gets you out of the self-protective frame of mind and back into the generative leadership frame of mind.

The Big Question, in other words, changes your story from the realm of your life alone to the LIFE you share with everyone. It takes whatever dilemma you're facing out of an imaginary hermit's cave and plops it down in the village square, the real social unit where you actually live. This is a powerful question that will automatically reframe every story.

Pondering what LIFE is asking of you is a wonderfully bold question. It presumes that your own life is powerful enough that it can actually make a contribution to LIFE itself.

In a way, what neuroscience is teaching us is that all situations and circumstances are bundles of events. And events come from a merging of individual stories. And stories reflect beliefs. And beliefs, stored in the catacombs of the psyche, exist in little synaptic storage units that shape us—until we shape them.

Choosing to reconsider your beliefs, and reframe your stories, is the ultimate act of courage, resilience and resourcefulness.

It is the highest responsibility, and greatest pleasure, of leadership.

CHAPTER NINE

2.7 SECONDS

**Bull-riding requires a fire in the belly.
So does Quicksilver leadership.**

⬲

"Be bold, and mighty forces will come to your aid."
—GOETHE

IT'S A CLICHÉ that most of us take too long to figure out
that life is for real. And that it's far shorter than we realize.
And much sweeter than we dream.

That's what country music star Tim McGraw sings about
in "Live Like You Were Dying," his ballad to a father dying
young. The lyrics celebrate the decision to live intensely in
the face of death.

What did you do when you got the diagnosis? the trouba-
dour wants to know—*Man, what'd you do*?

The father answers in the triumphal refrain that makes
the song an anthem to life. *I went sky divin,' I went Rocky
Mountain climbin,' I went two point seven seconds on a bull
named Fu Manchu.*

The dying father's wish for his son seems shocking: *Some
day I hope you get the chance to live like you were dying.*

We all have our Fu Manchus. They're the countless
nameless fears that run us. In so many ways, most of them

unconscious, we tend to dodge those fears. The evasion cuts deep synaptic ruts inside us. We stick to those ruts because we think they keep us safe. We get comfortable with them. That's tragic, because they often lead us away from where we really want to go. Much of the time they keep leaders from leading and the rest of us from living like we were dying.

What I think we come to fear as much as anything—deep down, quietly but resolutely—is leaving the path we know for ones we don't.

Thoreau said that most of us lead lives of quiet desperation and that we go to our graves with the song still in us. Why would we do that?

The synaptic ruts of fear, I think.

And what I think we come to fear as much as anything—deep down, quietly but resolutely—is leaving the path we know for ones we don't.

Step out of that rut and there's some Fu Manchu waiting for you. He paws the earth, nostrils flaring, bunched muscles twitching in the sun.

"Make my day," snorts Fu Manchu.

I don't recommend you try stepping out of the rut without that fire in your belly. You probably won't make it.

It takes more than guts to face him. It takes a good reason. It takes fire in the belly.

I'll tell you right now, I don't recommend you try stepping out of the rut without that fire in your belly. You probably won't make it. And that will just make you more comfortable with the ruts. And then you'll lose your faith in dreams. And there goes hope. And hope, remember, is the thing with feathers. It's also fire, pure flame. Lose hope and you'll enslave yourself to your own fears. That's what quiet desperation is. It takes a million forms, and in twenty-five years of executive coaching I've seen a lot of them and the toll they take on leaders and their organizations.

So if the fire's not there, you've got to build it first. Kindle it, breathe on it, fuel it, fan the flames—I have found that chin-high is about the right height. You need that much heat to drive you out of your ruts.

"Nothing is so much to be feared as fear," Thoreau also said. "Atheism may comparatively be popular with God himself."

Fire in the belly is what will send those fears up in smoke. God, Thoreau seemed to suggest, loves a good fear-burning fire in the belly. Whether you lead a multi-billion dollar corporation, as some of my clients do, or a nation, or a department, or a team, or a family, or just yourself, I can't emphasize strongly enough how important it is to nurse your fire and keep it stoked.

One way or another we're all leaders, but if you are actually paid to lead others—please think about this—you aren't *authorized* to lead a life of quiet desperation. Or go to your grave with your song unsung. It's not in your contract. You get paid to sing like Rick Rescorla.

The record shows that Rescorla was among the greatest platoon leaders in U.S. Army history. He sang to his troops, literally, during the battle of Ia Drang, one of the bloodiest of the Vietnam War. The great Lt. Rescorla rallied the boys depending on him in a black moment. He lifted their spirits and brought them out of a valley of death.

Rescorla later became first vice president for security for Morgan Stanley Dean Witter. When he evacuated the twenty-seven hundred souls entrusted to him from the World Trade Center after the September 11 terrorist attack, saving all their lives, trading his own for theirs, he sang to them as he guided them down the stairs. Rick Rescorla went to his grave, as we all can if we choose, singing at the top of his lungs. (He was a Cornishman and he sang old Cornish fighting songs.) You can read about him in the books, *We Were Soldiers Once... and Young,* and *Heart of a Soldier.*

Quiet desperation is not unknown among senior executives (we're all familiar with the sad stories of the occasional stress-induced suicide), but I would say my clients are less prone to it than needless suffering. Their suffering results from trying to meet the endless challenges they face from the synaptic ruts that imprison them. To escape those ruts they need practices. They hire me to coach them out of their unique ruts by tailoring practices to meet their specific needs. Among the practices I teach are the ones included for you in this book.

Dr. Ida Critelli Schick, a professor of health services administration who is one of the people I asked to review this book, made a critical observation about these practices. She said that they only "*appear* simple. They are not. I would judge them to be difficult to sustain without support. I would suggest that an individual would need tremendous discipline to stay with and to complete the exercises in a productive way. H/she would need someone to guide and encourage and re-direct when necessary."

I think most of my clients would agree with Dr. Schick. That's why they often have my colleagues and me work with them for two, three, four, five years.

Such are the demands of the modern marketplace that I think it is simply impossible for organizations to perform optimally without an effective executive coaching support system like this in place. (Yes, I have my own coach.) No sports organization would dream of fielding a team without a good coaching staff. Neither do I believe should any company.

But I want to add an important caveat to Dr. Schick's point. All a coach can do is *offer* help. Effective coaches have a veritable arsenal of help to offer, but they can't make people accept their offer. No coach, as much as he or she might want to, can build a fire for you. Think of three of the greatest athletes of all time: Michael Jordan, Tiger Woods, Lance Armstrong. Their God-given gifts without their burning desire to use them would have been for naught. The same is true of the leaders I coach. Life is so utterly personal.

I would say that if you are now leading an organization, and you and your top team do not have a personal coaching system in place designed to fit your specific needs, you are severely compromised. Not just for your sake, but also for the sake of a world that needs your best performance, I urge you to correct this situation as quickly as possible.

> This raises one of the most important paradoxes of leadership: it's not about you. And yet it is.

You can also apply the practices in this book to your personal life—*if* you choose. You can do this at any stage of life, as I know very well from my own experience. Not just for your sake, but also for the sake of a world that needs the best you have to offer, I urge you to do so. The practices offered here are intended to give you just the sort of guidance, encouragement, and redirection Dr. Schick refers to.

In any case, whether you're the President of the United States, the CEO of General Motors, or just someone privately facing the challenges of today's quicksilver world, fire in the belly is up to you. Don't leave home without it.

This raises one of the most important paradoxes of leadership: it's not about you. And yet it is. It's always about you, because leadership depends on your mastery of the ability to systematically escape your limitations—face your Fu Manchus—so you can lead others to do the same. Again, this is because you can't lead anyone anywhere except by going there first yourself. You can only bring out the best in others by constantly striving to bring out the best in you.

Fu Manchu is rideable, but not without fire in the belly. How do I know? Because I'm privileged to have some great bull riders among my clients. I get to rodeo with them all the time. And I'm a pretty good bull rider myself. And I'll tell you something else: I *love* it. Bull riding is life. It beats the hell out of the alternative.

The following anecdote illustrates how riding Fu Manchu plays out in the lives of my clients. This is a true account. I'm not going to name names, of course, but I don't have to otherwise worry about preserving anonymity, because events like this happen every day in the rodeo of my company's coaching assignments.

This particular client had completed the phase of his work that made him *intellectually* familiar with the concept of defensive routines. Remember, those are the reactive default settings we all have when we're under stress. By "intellectually familiar," I mean he now understood he even had such a thing and how it operated in his particular case. He wasn't yet practiced in mastering it, however. You might call this Fu Manchu ground school. The next step, of course, is climbing onto the bull's back.

Again, an essential part of our coaching is to be present during meetings, conference calls, etc., and sometimes, if asked, to offer facilitation. (Tiger Woods' coach has to watch Tiger Woods play.)

On this particular day, a coaching session was just ending when an important call came in from one of my client's senior subordinates. In the spirit of our coaching engagement, he asked if he could put the call on speakerphone so I could observe. The caller and I agreed. When the call ended, my client asked for my feedback.

That's what learning to ride Fu Manchu looks like. Zoological understanding of the beast is one thing. Incorporating that understanding into your experience, bones, and nerve cells is quite another.

"Well, that conversation actually took about thirty-eight minutes," I said. "In that thirty-eight minutes, you got triggered and interrupted her in a very dominant way eleven times."

"What?" he said.

I held up my notepad.

I reminded him that one of his defensive routines is to forcefully interrupt people until they submit.

His face went white. "Oh, shit," he said.

That's what learning to ride Fu Manchu looks like. Zoological understanding of the beast is one thing. Incorporating that understanding into your experience, bones, and nerve cells is quite another.

What will come next in this client's progress, assuming he has the fire in the belly to continue (and I think he does), is that every time he feels a defensive routine triggered, he will be able to quickly retrieve his mind back from that dark and lonely place that's often full of anger and upset. He will then be able to recast, reframe, reboot, re-aim, and quickly bounce back into the game of generative leadership. Doing that in two point seven seconds isn't out of the question.

When that starts to happen, the rewiring of his brain will be well and truly begun. His leadership skills will have been transformed. He will bring new possibilities into the world that are at this moment unimaginable.

TO BUILD A FIRE

THE CHANCES ARE VERY GOOD, certainly better than even, that at this moment you do not have a fire in your belly hot enough to ride Fu Manchu. It's perfectly obvious, for instance, that those most directly involved in the creation of Wall Street's Monster didn't.

So how do you build the kind of fire I'm talking about? Once again, it's pretty simple. Fortunately, in this case, it's easy, too. You do it with attention and intention. You do it with focused personal desire that capitalizes on the same powerful, survival-based neurological mechanisms that drive you to such pleasurable activities as eating and making love.

Attention addresses what you're anxious, worried, scared, angry about right now. Intention is about your most intense dreams, desires, hopes, longings. Combine the two *consciously*, and you put your mind in launch mode. Couple them with the practices in this book, and you're instantly in action in a way that will let you manage both the velocity and trajectory of the launch.

There is a feature in the hottest new Porsches called "launch control." It utilizes an exotic race-derived dual driveshaft manual/automatic transmission. Push the button on the dash to select the function. Foot on brake. Accelerator to floor.

> Launching a Porsche is sedate compared to launching your mind. Launching your mind is harder, though. How bad do you want it...?

The engine spools to sixty-five hundred RPM.

Now release the brake. The car becomes a slingshot.

In as little as three point six seconds you're screaming down the road at sixty miles an hour. That's fast, of course, but not as fast as two point seven seconds.

Launching a Porsche is sedate compared to launching your mind. Launching your mind is harder, though. *How bad do you want it...?*

It's almost a cinch that at this moment you can't list your top ten fears and goals. It's not in the nature of consciousness to be able to do that.

If you doubt it, imagine that a genie comes to you and says something like: "I'll make your ten worst worries and fears disappear, and I'll give you the ten things you want most. Two catches. First, you have to believe in me. Second, once you decide, you can't change your mind. So take your time."

This may seem as simplistic as the other exercises in this book, but, as you'll quickly discover if you give it a try, something like that genie actually exists. Scientists call the genie "attentional bias." Dr. Kessler writes about it in Chapter 8 of *The End of Overeating*. Attentional bias, he explains, is a function of our body's pain management system, our complex opiate receptors. We're biologically wired to seek pleasure. The experience of physical pleasure is supplied by the neurotransmitter dopamine. We incline toward pleasurable actions because of the little squirt of dopamine they give us.

> The kind of fire in the belly I'm talking about here is a "highly rewarding stimuli" of your own creation—a thought, an image, a goal, a reminder.

Writes Kessler: "Defined as 'the exaggerated amount of attention that is paid to highly rewarding stimuli at the expense of other (neutral) stimuli,' attentional bias allows us to pick out what matters most so we can pursue it."

The kind of fire in the belly I'm talking about here is a "highly rewarding stimuli" of your own creation—a thought, an image, a goal, a reminder.

For me, such a stimulus is the picture in my mind of angels—my unborn grandchildren. I can close my eyes and see them anytime I choose. I can meet with them in my mind and remind them I await them.

For Mark Shunk, it is the memory of laying down his figurative two-hundred-pound rock-filled backpack and helping others do the same.

For Larry Shook, it is another kind of memory. As Larry writes in the Epilogue, he flew in helicopter gunships in Vietnam. On the afternoon of January 1, 1968, he was readying his ship for a mission when Richard Lakin (nickname Lucky) approached and offered to take the mission for him. Larry accepted the offer. Lucky and two others did not survive the mission. Larry has run his fingers over Lucky's name on the Vietnam Memorial Wall. The memory of the man, and of the feeling of the chiseled letters of his name, is a dependable fire in Larry's belly, reminder that he has promises to keep.

What's your "highly rewarding stimuli?"

CAPTAIN SKI

**Great Leadership in a Time of Great
Confusion—A Personal Memory**

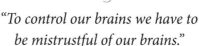

*"To control our brains we have to
be mistrustful of our brains."*
—DR. JAMES LECKMAN, *Yale University School of Medicine*

THE ARGUMENT OF THIS BOOK is that all of us today
face an urgent mandate to wake up, to become "conscious."
As this book defines it, becoming conscious means learning
how to distrust our thoughts, while trusting our ability to
think about them, and then choosing thoughts that best suit
us. This isn't about what is usually referred to as "positive
thinking." It's about "responsible thinking" instead. And not
responsible in the moral sense. Responsible in the pragmatic
sense. No one is responsible for our thoughts but us.

To contest that proposition is to waste one's life. That's
Michael O'Brien's perspective. I share it so passionately that
I've taken my best shot at helping him with this book.

Whether we choose to wake up just for ourselves, or for
the sake of the relationships and organizations we lead, this
is probably the central business of our lives. We're either in
the responsible thinking business or we're not. Our thoughts

take us where we're going, but they come from where we've been. And where we've been often isn't where we want to remain, or return. I think this is true for the individual and the species.

Change or die. That seems to be Mother Nature's motto.

If you think about it, the whole point of "leading" anyone anywhere is to reflect deeply on the most important destinations and the best way to reach them, and then to step out and go first.

Leaders must go first, insists Dr. O'Brien.

In their executive coaching practice, Michael O'Brien and his partners have been making this argument for the last twenty-five years. Their clients like the argument because it helps them lead better. As Mark Shunk says, it helps them discover the powerful truth of who they really are. Mark and Abe Lincoln seem to agree—we really do have better angels in our nature. We just have to give them a chance.

Making this argument in book form, however, is very different from making it face-to-face. When Michael and his colleagues coach, the context of their assignment is built in, supplied by the specific needs of their clients. This book had to create its own context in order to meet your needs, if the argument was to have a prayer of doing you any good.

I returned home from interviewing Michael in March of 2008 looking for a context capable of illustrating why consciousness, as Michael teaches it, might matter to you. I didn't have to look very hard. The March 23, 2008, *New York Times* story, "What Created This Monster?" made it clear that a Chernobyl-like meltdown of the world's economy was underway. It offered the perfect illustration of why we can no longer afford the pandemic sleepwalking that has passed for too long as modern leadership. You probably don't need much convincing at this point that Wall Street's Monster menaces not just you, but your children, and perhaps theirs as well— *unless*, that is, our current breakdown triggers a breakthrough equal to its size.

So far, as a story in the May 18, 2009, issue of *The New Yorker* suggested, no such breakthrough is in sight. Called "The Death of Kings: Notes from a Meltdown," the article portrayed a world turned upside down.

"This thing we're in doesn't yet have a name," pronounced author Nick Paumgarten. He compared the crisis to "a plague or a war," except that such comparisons trivialized the "thing's" true character. Paumgarten recited a litany of causes leading to the "spectacular collapse. To tell the story of them all, in the proper context and detail, will require an Edward Gibbon. The fall of Rome, by comparison, was a local event."

Neither Paumgarten nor his many sources seemed able to catch their breaths enough to put into words the chaos they observed. "Mad Max time, baby," quipped one financier, a reference to the Mel Gibson apocalypse movie.

I have known a world of such pandemonium. It was called Vietnam.

In 1967 and 1968, the deadliest years of the war, I was a door gunner and crew chief on a helicopter gunship in the Mekong Delta. Our aviation company's "slicks," the troop-transporting aircraft, carried American and South Vietnamese infantrymen into and out of battle. Our gunships covered those insertions, then provided close air support for the "grunts" below as they conducted their operations.

"Cover" is one of those bloodless euphemisms like "collateral damage." It means we shot at the people who were shooting at the slicks, shooting at "our" troops, shooting at us. There was blood—sometimes enough to turn brown water red. We also covered the inevitable "dust-offs," the medical evacuations of the wounded and dead. Sometimes we couldn't suppress the enemy fire enough to get the dust-offs in, and the wounded died. And then we covered the extractions.

In these air cavalry operations, it wasn't unusual for us to ferry the grunts from one battle site to another in the course of long days that began in cool mornings and ran through burning heat (heat prostration was a common casualty in Vietnam; we'd dust off a guy as quickly for it as for a bullet wound) into hot, muggy nights.

It took me three months of my twelve-month Vietnam tour to get transferred into aviation. The Army tried to make an MP out of me, but I had given up my student deferment to volunteer for the draft, volunteer for Vietnam, volunteer for combat. I didn't intend to be a cook, clerk or MP. My father had been a Marine in the Pacific during WW II; I was raised to believe that if the country was at war, then the place for its young men was fighting in that war.

That was my story, Michael O'Brien would say. Of course it never would have occurred to me in those days to think of it that way. I was living THE story, not MY story. How could there be any doubt of the "reality" of the Vietnam War?

Anyway, I didn't go to Vietnam heroically. It turned out that I was so scared that a few nights before I left I was embarrassed to find myself crying in the arms of a sweet young woman. Who ever heard of John Wayne or Randolph Scott doing something like that?

In nine months, I logged twelve hundred combat hours. Twice my aircraft was disabled by ground fire and we were forced into dicey landings. Once, in the middle of the night, we were shot out of the sky. The ship took so many hits it sounded like someone had thrown gravel at it.

We were all hunters. We were all hunted. Nothing about the Vietnam War I experienced conformed to the Hollywood and television depictions of war I had been raised on. Vietnam was certainly not my father's Oldsmobile. I had a careening, hundred-mile-an-hour, fifty-yard-line seat on the whole grim, confused business.

I tell you this because it makes visual a portion of my own particular neural landscape that no MRI ever could. This is a swath of the terrain I brought to my attempt to assist Dr. O'Brien with this book. I consider this relevant to the central point of *Quicksilver*, which is that we all have to play the hand life deals us. *How* we play that hand—well, that, fortunately, is a blessedly, fascinatingly, different matter. The options are infinite.

The picture of me in the back of this book was taken at Mesa Verde National Park, in Colorado. I share it as a metaphor. You can see the dramatic story of time etched in the landscape. Meander down into the canyons and you'll find another story, a silent tale told in the hidden cliff dwellings and middens and stone tools of the long-lost Anasazi people. You can't see the modern stories in the landscape of the mind of the man in the foreground, me, but they are present as surely as the lingering ghosts of Mesa Verde behind me. My stories form a kind of parietal art in the canyons of my brain. It's the same for all of us. We're all mysterious walking epics of the universe.

As with everyone who goes to war, my memories of it breathe in me and will until I die. They influence my intense desire to help Michael make this book as useful to you as possible. I'm going to give you a glimpse of my Vietnam because of how I relate it to this book and the spectacular moment of history those of us alive now share. First, let me make something clear: I do not consider war glorious. Quite the opposite. It kills the best of us and wounds the rest of us.

The greatest leader I have ever known was Harry Gawkowski. He was the pale, slight, twenty-six-year-old captain who led our gun platoon, the Mustangs. Captain Ski was Mustang Six.

He was the furthest thing from a physically imposing man, except for one thing: his demeanor. He exuded command bearing, because he exuded purpose. There wasn't a distracted bone in Captain Ski's body. Ski's focus alone created an energy field around him.

It was my privilege to crew for many fine pilots, but Ski was in a class of his own. He flew a helicopter gunship the way Michael Jordon played basketball. The night I was blown out of the sky, Ski had the stick. Dave Holloway, our platoon's instructor pilot, was co-pilot. If those two gentlemen hadn't been in control, I don't believe this particular piece of neural cave art, this living memory, would exist. We would have all blinked out of the world to become names on the Wall.

The secret to Captain Ski's greatness as a leader, though, at least as I saw it then and still do all these years later, went beyond his mere skills into the ineffable zone of example. Ski *led* us. He didn't so much order or tell us as *show* us. To be the best Mustang you could be, you simply followed Ski.

"How the hell do we do this, sir?"

"Follow me."

To lead as Ski did involves action that flows from being. Orders, edicts, rhetoric hardly figure in it at all.

Life in a helicopter gunship in Vietnam was sensory. There was the scenery, which often included rising tracer fire, and violent motion—no roller coaster ride could compare; I puked my guts out until I got used to it. Rich radio communication filled your headset, so you always knew how bad things were around you. Some of our missions were in places so bad, they triggered gallows humor when we saw their names scrawled on the operations chalkboard.

We're goin' to DONG TAM, we would growl like blues singers. *Ain't nevah comin' back!*

Day after day, from first light to last, Ski led us to work in this hostile, chaotic environment with a calm that you couldn't believe without experiencing it. The "Father Knows Best/Ozzie and Harriet" verities of my world had been shattered. They were replaced by the unblinking truthfulness of a twenty-six-year-old who knew that all you can do is your best. And that verity trumped the illusions of my lost world. It still does.

Once you experienced Ski's world, it rewired you. A split second into a mission with Ski was all it took to teach you that your job wasn't about you. It was about the guys on the ground you were trying to help. That was it. That was my whole world. For me, there was no "Vietnam War," no "domino theory," no global politics, no history, no future. When we did our jobs, those guys on the ground got to go home—or at least they got another crack at it.

So if flying with Ski suited you (and it didn't everyone), the paradox of the job was its serenity. Also, its shockingly rich return on investment. When you join your life to something bigger, you find that it suddenly means more than it ever could otherwise. You don't ever want to revert to the previous, smaller version. Loss of the bigger life would be unbearable. Ski didn't talk much, but that's what he managed to teach me.

The Mustangs were picky about who they let in. And once you were a Mustang, you could change your mind and stop anytime you wanted. Some guys did. We didn't hold it against them. You didn't want anybody up there in those ships who didn't mean it. That commitment, I believe most of us found, somehow built upon itself. I'm still finding this out more than forty years later.

I'm not sure everything I've done since flying with Captain Ski would measure up to his standards. Even so, he's still leading me. He always will. That's the galvanic power of the great leader. It is as eternal as the beat of the human heart.

The way out of our current crises, I believe, is to be found in the star map of our neurons. I don't think we're lost at all. I think we just have to open our eyes, figure out what matters, commit to acting on it, and roll in. Would that young Captain Ski could lead us all. I really don't think it's any more complicated than that.

If that makes sense to you, I believe the practices contained in this book can help you engage with your commitment and sustain that engagement. Pick an exercise. Do it. Repeat. Continue.

Your engagement, I have no doubt, will change our world for the better.

In the helicopters, in Vietnam, when we departed at dawn for our missions, there was this ritual. We would start the engines. The air would blur in the heat of the exhaust. And then, in our headsets, there would be this call and response check of the radios to make sure we could hear one another. Our voices, our ability to speak and listen—that was our salvation.

Each aircraft commander would state his call sign, then say, "Fox Mike (for FM), UHF, VHF." And then the next aircraft in line would follow. If someone's radio was broken, it was quickly replaced. It was beautiful, a kind of rosary. "Hail Mary, Mother of torque, we're all together." And then the AC, the aircraft commander, would say over his intercom, "Comin' up." And the door gunner would look around to make sure we weren't going to run into anything on his side of the aircraft, and say, "Clear right." And the crew chief would do the same and say, "Clear left."

And then the entire lift, eighteen slicks and four gunships, would go to work together in the Southeast Asian dawn. In the midst of the darkest thing humanity does, that connectedness was as beautiful as a Gregorian chant.

Clear left.

QUICKSILVER QUICKLY

Three Simple Steps

THE FOLLOWING IS OFFERED as a Master Practice for this book. It's a checklist for what to do when you're seriously stumped—the Apollo 13 protocol.

"Work the problem, people," NASA flight director Gene Kranz famously told his Mission Control team after cascading failures left three astronauts stranded in space.

Conscious leadership, beginning with conscious leadership of oneself, is a kind of permanent Apollo 13 mission. It's hardest when you need it the most.

As with any checklist, using Quicksilver Quickly is straightforward.

STEP 1 — **Take any worry, conflict, crisis or break-down and select a practice to apply to it.**

STEP 2 — **Review the Quicksilver Principles.**

STEP 3 — **Use the practice you've chosen, coupled with the principles, to "work the problem."**

That will get you home.

Quicksilver Principles

- As a leader, you're accountable—no matter what.

- As the owner of your life, you're the only one who really leads it. Your every thought, feeling, and action are expressions of leadership.

- As a leader, you go first. When Life demands a change of heart or mind, you must first change yourself before you can change the hearts and minds of others.

- If you don't have your mind, it will have you. (Your perceptions are of your own making.)

- Don't resist resistance. What you resist persists.

- When things aren't working as you'd like, look for the fear that is always lurking, first in yourself, then in others. Because…

- Fear unnoticed and unmanaged trumps reason.

- Courage is the mastery of fear, not its absence.

- Ideology, a kind of volunteer slavery, is the death of creative leadership.

- What is most personal about you is frequently *not* private. Your emotions, especially when you're under stress, are constantly telegraphed to those around you.

- Because leadership occurs in relationships, leaders bring consciousness into their conversations.

- As a leader, you work with what is so. You transform what is so into what could be.

List of Practices

ACCOUNTABILITY   77
Change Shoulds to Coulds
Don't let the past determine your future

COURAGE
Breathe
Oxygen fuels your emotional intelligence   94

Tell Yourself a Story
Take charge of your mind's greatest power   96

AUTHENTICITY
Evaluate a Stuck Relationship   117
Navigate beyond your fear toward your principles

Be Complete with Incompletion   118
Live well, with some things unfinished

INTENTIONALITY
Discover Your Defensive Routines: 143
Fight & Flight
Learn to notice when you've been hijacked

Have a Breakthrough Conversation   146
See the other person's story

Scout for Organizational Defensive Routines   148
Discuss (gulp) the unmentionable

Move Beyond Bad Moods, Quickly   150
Notice and lay down your burdens

CREATE THE TRUTH
Keep a "Snake List"   167
Awareness and good technique stop your
problems from biting you

Be Interested vs. Interesting   168
Really, try it. You'll become interesting

Turn Complaints Into Requests   168
End a lot of suffering

Depose Ideology   169
Taking a stand is way more powerful

Explore the Heart of Conflict with   171
Constructive Dialogue
Develop a nimble mind that creates empathy

CAPITALIZE ON MESSES
Ask Yourself a "Paradoxical   187
Development Question"
Unleash the *über* problem-solver within

Ask Yourself What You Need   189
Illuminate your secret yearnings so you can get
them met

Ask for Forgiveness
Liberate yourself from past mistakes   191

Ask Yourself the Biggest Question of All
When you know the answer, you can truly lead   192

AUTHORS' BIOS

DR. MICHAEL O'BRIEN is president of the O'Brien Group, an executive coaching consultancy with an international clientele. Widely recognized for his expertise in the role played by personal psychology in leadership and change management, he has conducted hundreds of seminars and given numerous keynote presentations on the subject in the course of a twenty-five-year career. He has contributed articles to many professional publications and is author of *Profit from Experience: A guide to knowing yourself and influencing others* (1995, now in a fourth edition, Sombrero Press). Dr. O'Brien's clientele includes such companies as NYNEX, Bayer, AT&T, Xerox, Prudential, Convergys, Sun Life, Catholic Healthcare Partners, New York Life, Procter & Gamble and many others. He holds a Master's Degree in Education and a Doctorate in Human Resources Development.

LARRY SHOOK is a veteran journalist, publisher, editor and communications consultant. He has written for such publications as *The New York Times, The Washington Post,* and *Newsweek.* His reporting has won several of the nation's top journalism awards. He co-authored *Profit from Experience* with Dr. O'Brien.

For more information, go to www.obriengroup.us